Donnie
BASEBALL

The **Definitive** Biography
of **Don Mattingly**

Mike Shalin

TRIUMPH
B O O K S

Triumph Books and colophon are registered trademarks of Random House, Inc.

Library of Congress Cataloging-in-Publication Data

Shalin, Mike, 1954–
  Donnie baseball : the definitive biography of Don Mattingly / Mike Shalin.
    p. cm.
  ISBN 978-1-60078-536-8
  1. Mattingly, Don, 1961– 2. Baseball players—United States—Biography.
I. Title.
  GV865.M374S53 2011
  796.357092—dc22
  [B]
                        2010051181

This book is available in quantity at special discounts for your group or organization. For further information, contact:

Triumph Books
542 South Dearborn Street
Suite 750
Chicago, Illinois 60605
(312) 939-3330
Fax (312) 663-3557
www.triumphbooks.com

Printed in U.S.A.
ISBN: 978-1-60078-536-8
Design by Patricia Frey

To Mary, my significantly better half, and to my boys—
Josh, Taylor, and Mac. You four are the reason for everything!

To my brothers, who taught me anything about sports worth knowing.

To Mom and Dad—you are both gone but never *forgotten.*

To Ted Baxter—you will always be an inspiration.

Contents

Foreword

I have never heard anybody say a single negative thing about Donnie.

The first thing I noticed about him was that he was only concerned about getting attention for the way he played, and not from any kind of theatrics. He was just a guy who went out there and played the game, nuts and bolts.

When I got the Yankees job in '96, I didn't know that '95 would end up his last season. I don't think anybody knew for sure what was going to happen—if he was going to come back or not. When he decided to retire, I wasn't sure if it was sort of forced on him. Then after I got to know him a little bit, I realized that his back was such an issue for him that he couldn't continue playing.

In 1997 he came to spring training as one of the "celebrity instructors." I saw right away that he was something more than that. He put in his time, went out and worked with the hitters (of course with my hitting coach at the time, with his permission), and he was pretty darn impressive to me. In fact, when he came in to say good-bye that first spring, I said to him, "Donnie, just let me know when you're ready to do this. We'll make a spot for you." I noticed his skills as a baseball person right away. To me, he was a superstar. And for him to walk in and not use his superstar status to get something for nothing really impressed me.

When I first saw him it was clear to me that he could coach. He had plenty of energy, and he had something to say. I may have told him that first year, "I know you can coach at this level, and I think if you want to go beyond that and manage, you'll be able to do that." I had met him before, but that spring was the first time I had been around him for a period of time. It really made me appreciate him for much more than what we knew he could do on the field.

After the 2003 season, we wanted to make some changes on our staff. George Steinbrenner, Brian Cashman, and I were in a meeting and talking about who we were going to get to replace hitting coach Rick Down. I think it was George who raised it: "What about Donnie?" I said that would be perfect for me, but it depended on whether or not Donnie was ready to come back.

George said, "Well, I'll talk to him." Evidently he made the job appealing to Donnie, because I know he was still tied to his kids at that time and had to be around for them. George made it right with Donnie and made it convenient for him to go home when he needed to. Donnie, aside from having great character, is a very responsible individual. When he felt he had to do something, he was going to do it. It didn't matter how much money you offered him. It was always about what he felt in his heart that he had to do.

When he came on as coach, the players gravitated toward him right away. I thought I knew a lot about hitting, but to this day he will have me looking at things I never thought to look at. I can see things, but he connects the dots to tell you why something is happening and why a certain guy is having a problem, and it's usually something that I haven't noticed. He's really good. He has really studied the hitting part of it. In New York, he moved from hitting coach to bench coach. After I left the Yankees, he called me when he heard the rumors I was going to the Dodgers. He said, "If I don't get this job [as manager of the Yankees], would you take me with you?" I told him I'd love for him to come with me.

I wanted him as my hitting coach, and I told him that the position would not retard his opportunities to become a manager or learn about managing. In fact, he's my recommendation to take my place. It's going to be up to the ballclub to make the final decision, obviously. I know Ned Colletti feels very strongly about Donnie. Ned learned a lot about him over this past year. Donnie had an opportunity to go to a couple of other places last winter, and he and Ned talked about the prospects of staying in Los Angeles without Ned making him an out-and-out deal. Donnie wants to stay here.

He managed the team in spring training this year; I picked it up the last week. He managed the games, and I ran all the meetings. We may have had 30 to 35 players in spring training, not counting pitchers, and Donnie gave every single one of them the same attention. Whether it was Andre Ethier or Manny Ramirez or some guy you're never going to hear of, Donnie was always there with him first thing in the morning. That says a lot to me. In the games we play now he keeps his own lineup card. He follows double switches, then they make changes, and he does it on his card. So he's practicing.

To me, his communication skills are very strong. His believability and integrity are very strong. When he talks, he's saying something. There's nothing empty about him at all. He walks in and he wants nothing for nothing. He earns everything he gets. He's going to be outstanding as a manager. Now, is he going to trip and fall once in a while? Sure. But knowing who he is as a person, it's not going to be an issue.

—Joe Torre, then-manager, Los Angeles Dodgers, June 2010.
(Three months later, Mattingly was officially named
the Dodgers manager for the 2011 season.)

Acknowledgments

First and foremost, I would like to thank the subject of this book, Don Mattingly, who didn't want to write a book but was there to help me write one about him. Thanks, Donnie.

Thanks to all others who were more than willing to talk Donnie Baseball, starting with Joe Torre, who never hesitated in agreeing to do the foreword; to Baseball-Reference.com, for so many of the numbers used; to Jeff Idelson, Dick Bresciani, Chris Costello, Monica Barlow, Arthur Pincus, Joe Casale, Ray Schulte, as well as the YES Network and WFAN. Apologies to anyone I left out here.

Introduction

B ack in 1980, when things were still more than just a little crazy in the Bronx, someone among the Yankees brass called Bob Schaefer, the former minor league infielder who was managing the Greensboro Hornets of the newly named South Atlantic League. The Yankees had a kid who was a first baseman/outfielder who didn't project the power numbers usually connected to those positions, so they called Schaefer and suggested he give the kid a try at second base.

One hitch: the kid was left-handed.

An answer to the hitch? The kid was ambidextrous. He even started out throwing right-handed as a little boy. The second-base experiment was brief and never got past the early stages. The kid moved back to left field. Seventeen years later, that kid was enshrined in Monument Park at Yankee Stadium—as a first baseman.

The progeny of a hardworking Evansville, Indiana, family and the youngest of four brothers and a sister, Don Mattingly would eventually leave the outfield, move to first base, and become one of the great players in the Yankees' long and proud history. He hit .307 with 222 home runs and won nine Gold Gloves during 14 seasons. His production was cut short in the second half of his career by back misery, but his greatness never diminished.

Mattingly didn't get there the easy way. He wasn't a natural talent like a Ken Griffey Jr. or a Barry Bonds. He could always hit, but there were questions about the other aspects of his game. He worked, worked, and worked some more and wound up as the Yankees captain.

I covered the Yankees for the *New York Post* in 1981 and '82 and was there to see only the beginning of Mattingly's career in the Bronx—the first seven games (at the end of the '82 season), to be exact. But after moving to Boston and taking on the Red Sox beat, I got to know Mattingly over the years. Now, many years later, I gladly accepted the assignment to write a book on No. 23, the man they call "Donnie Baseball."

This is *not* an authorized biography. However, it should be pointed out that it is one that is being done with the full cooperation of the subject. Mattingly did not want to officially authorize what you're about to read because he didn't want to do his own book. There are also some stories in these pages related by others that Mattingly couldn't recall, so he elected to go this way.

But sitting down for two long sessions with Mattingly turned into much of what you are going to read. There are also many stories and feelings from others about a guy who seemingly doesn't have an enemy in baseball. In many ways, this book is an ode to Don Mattingly, something that developed because of the universal love for him in the baseball world.

If you are looking for controversy and negativity, you won't find much of it here, though Mattingly speaks frankly about George Steinbrenner and what happened amid the craziness of the Yankees of 1983–95. He harkens back to a career that saw him, one of the greatest players of his time, fall short of every player's ultimate dream of playing in and winning a World Series.

"Donnie Baseball." From Evansville, Indiana, all the way to Monument Park...and beyond.

"He was the most beloved athlete I've ever seen in New York," longtime Yankees radio announcer John Sterling said.

—Mike Shalin
September 2010

Chapter 1

The Road to the Bronx

"A star is a guy who has talent and intelligence. Donnie had both. He didn't have the talent when he first started. He had the tools to work with, but he made himself a good player. And I think guys who make themselves players like that appreciate the game more. I think they work harder and respect the game a lot more."

—Bob Schaeffer,
Mattingly's minor league manager at Greensboro

Yankees television broadcaster Michael Kay remembers the dreadful trip home from Seattle after the Yankees lost the 1995 American League Division Series to the Mariners—a series the Yanks led 2–0 before losing three straight in the Pacific Northwest.

"It was gut-wrenching," said Kay, who covered Mattingly both as a newspaper reporter and broadcaster, looking back at that fateful night. "We always refer to it as the Flying Funeral—everybody on that team was wracked with emotion since they lost and because that [playoff run] was for Mattingly."

In 1985 the Yankees won 97 games and had the second-best record in the American League—but there was no wild card to advance to the playoffs. The following year, they won 90 games but again fell just short of the postseason. In 1994 the Yankees were 6½ games ahead in the American League East when the season came to an end because of the labor dispute.

Finally in 1995, the Yankees came from behind and secured a spot in the playoffs as the American League's first wild card team, with Mattingly leading the way down the stretch. They then won the first two games of the first American League Division Series at Yankees Stadium. Mattingly remembers that the reception he received from the house when he came out to run sprints before the game was the greatest feeling he ever had as a player.

The Yankees flew out to Seattle needing just one win to advance. But Mattingly had already won his final game as a player. The Mariners won Games 3 and 4. The Yankees took a 5–4 lead in the top of the eleventh inning of Game 5, three innings after the Mariners nullified Mattingly's two-run sixth-inning double by scoring two in the eighth.

Ahead by a run, the end came quickly. In fact, it came in a span of just eight pitches. With Jack McDowell on the mound for New York, Joey Cora dropped down a bunt and just beat Mattingly to the bag for a hit. Two pitches later, Ken Griffey Jr. singled, with Cora taking third. Two pitches after that, Edgar Martinez rifled a double down the left-field line. Cora scored easily and a then-fleet Griffey came all the way around, sliding across the plate and ending Don Mattingly's career.

Then came the long flight home.

"I think that whole stretch drive was to get Mattingly to the World Series. Everybody knew that he wasn't going to play again. There was weeping on the plane. He was walking around, actually consoling people," Kay said. "Up and down the aisle, talking to people. Everybody was saying good-bye, but everybody was crushed because of him."

Radio broadcaster Suzyn Waldman was also on the plane. "The whole thing was heart-wrenching," she said. "It was horrible. Horrible. It was the worst plane ride I've ever had in my life."

Despite the Yankees losing the series, Mattingly went out in style. He hit .417 in the ALDS after finishing the regular season with a 10-game hitting streak. Mattingly had already told people he was done, but nothing was official. In fact, he didn't officially retire through the 1996 season. But he was done. The road had ended, and he never got to the promised land.

"I remember once he told me, 'Just getting to that series was enough for me,'" Kay said. "He said, 'Of course I'd have liked to have done more, but I always wondered how I would perform on the biggest stage [of postseason baseball], with all the pressure and all the lights on. And the fact that I did made me feel somewhat complete.' I'm just paraphrasing. He said, 'That's what was important to me, that I had an opportunity to play on that level.'"

* * *

Coach Quentin Merkel knew there was something different about the youngest of the four Mattingly sons. It was apparent at a very young age.

"My brother was in the same class as Don. They played Little League in the same place—North Little League Park—and when Donnie was 10 years old, he hit a number of home runs," Merkel said, looking back at the kid who would become his most famous product. "I played Little League when I was 12 years old, and I hit three and I thought that was pretty good. But there was no way I'd ever hit a home run as a 10-year-old. He was something special."

And Merkel, who is still coaching high school baseball, was at Reitz Memorial High School when Mattingly got there. He was clearly glad the kid was coming, and it didn't take long for the youngest of Bill and Mary Mattingly's five children to make an impression.

"In all the years that I've coached, I've only had a handful, maybe five or six young men, who played varsity ball as a freshman. With him, there wasn't any question about it. Normally I would have tryouts with the sophomores through seniors, but when he was a freshman, I had tryouts with freshmen through seniors," he laughed.

"I felt that he could play for us and could handle it and he did. He hit something like .350 as a freshman, and he got a number of clutch base hits that won ballgames for us. He hit over .400 as a sophomore, and in his last two years he hit over .500."

And Mattingly wasn't even playing his favorite sport.

"When I was a kid, I loved basketball more than anything," Mattingly said. "Football was my least favorite because it's not that much fun to get hit. I started liking it more in my junior year. I was a quarterback and a safety. But I didn't want to play in college.

"I really liked basketball more than any other sport growing up because you could go out and shoot, dribble, and practice by yourself. I was a point guard. I should have passed a lot more; I tried to score too much. Looking back, I would have been a lot better off passing a lot more often.

"Baseball kind of showed up and just ended up being what I was meant to do. I loved basketball, but I remember going to high school my freshman year. We had a pretty great baseball program—the coach has probably won more than 800 games now. My brother went there after his Catholic school closed. He went to Reitz Memorial in his senior year, and the baseball team was fourth in the state.

"They were known for baseball, and they were in the top 10 every year. Merkel had a reputation for being a drill sergeant type. I remember one of the first baseball meetings. School ended at something like 2:45, and the baseball meeting was scheduled for 3:00 in a certain room. When 3:00 came he closed the door and locked it. When guys came and knocked on the door, he'd just say, 'I'll see you next year.'

"You'd see if the kid really wanted to play. If he hung on and said, 'Hey, Coach, my bad,' Merkel would say, 'Okay, I'll give you a shot.' But if you didn't, if you just gave up and left, then you were out. He was that kind of coach. But he came to me in my freshman year, I remember I was in my gym class, and said, 'I'm going to put you on the varsity team this year.'

"I didn't know that he knew who I was. I'd won a batting title in the Babe Ruth League the year before. But I didn't know if he'd seen me play. Maybe he knew me from my brother."

The coach's decision turned out to be a wise one.

"During those four years, I think we only lost about eight ballgames," Merkel said. "In Mattingly's junior and senior years, we were 59–1 and that one loss was the state championship game. We won it when he was a junior and we were 30–0. Going into the state championship game [during Mattingly's senior year] we were 29–0, and we lost it in 10 innings.

"He was a tremendous hitter and a tremendous fielder—and he was very smart. He was probably one of the most coachable kids I've ever had. You could tell him something or show him something one time, and you didn't have to drill him 50 times. He had it, he'd pick it up."

It doesn't surprise Merkel that Mattingly's career went from playing to coaching.

"He's very smart, he's got a tremendous memory—I don't think the guy forgets anything—I think he will do a good job, if he gets an opportunity [to manage]."

One thing Mattingly learned in high school was that you can't get too upset when you don't get hits. There are times when you hit the ball hard and get nothing for it. Merkel said Mattingly had two triples in the state championship game his junior year and hit the ball just as well and got nothing in the championship loss in the following season.

"We won it all my junior year, we won the state finals," Mattingly recalled. "I crushed the ball, got a lot of hits. My senior year we got beat in the finals. In the last two games of that tournament 1 must have lined out six or seven times. I mean, I hit everything on the nose. I look back and I was like one-for-something. I wonder, what would I do differently? I wouldn't do anything different."

It was a philosophy he kept with him throughout his career, and one he used with his hitters as their coach.

Merkel recalled Mattingly's strengths as a hitter. "In high school, from a hitting standpoint—this will be my 42nd year coaching high school baseball this year—I've never had a kid who could hit a ball as hard as consistently as Donnie could. Boy, he was just something special. A big problem with young players is that when they get in a tough situation, a pressure situation, most of them have trouble with it. But [Mattingly] relished situations like that. He wanted to get up to the plate, and usually when he got up there he got something done."

Mattingly can remember when it got serious for him, when he thought this might be the sport for him.

"We were rated first or second in the state to start [my freshman] year," he said. "I was playing the outfield. That year I had a pretty decent year—hit three-something, which for a freshman is okay. I played Legion in the summer, which was at that point pretty good baseball. We were going over to Henderson to play a game early and then over to Owensboro, [Kentucky], because they had a guy pitching over there who was the Reds' No. 1 pick and was signing the next day. [Mark King was] pitching that night against us.

"We played the game in Henderson and drove about 40 minutes to the other place and it was packed. It was electric. I was 15 years old and I went 2-for-3 off this guy with two doubles in the gap. From that point on I got letters from the Cincinnati scout. I thought I was going to Cincinnati because that was where my first letter came from. I didn't know the system or how it worked. Then when Detroit was in town, I thought they would probably take me. I ended up going to the Yankees, and I didn't even know those guys came to see me.

"After that day is when I really started working," he said. "I always worked, but [after that] I really put in an effort.... I started doing stuff in my basement, trying to build up my wrist and arms. I hit all the time. When I worked it was different. It was toward that goal. When I got that first letter, I knew I wanted to play baseball."

The college offers came. He committed to Indiana State but wound up signing with the Yankees after being taken in the 19th round.

"My dad wanted me to go to school," he said. "I'll tell you how dumb I was in those days, really. I was in Indiana, getting recruited by Miami and Florida State and thinking, *Why would I want to go down there to play baseball?* But Indiana State had a coach who was like our high school coach—really tough. [Larry] Bird had gone there, close to home. I chose Terre Haute, Indiana, over Miami—it's just not right."

As it ended up, neither was college—at least that's the way Mattingly felt. So instead of college, he signed with the Yankees.

"I think I signed for $23,500," he said. "That was the bonus for a 19th-round pick. And I think I got that incentive bonus, too. It was something like $7,500. You get so much at every level."

Jax Robertson and Gust Poulos were the Yankees scouts who got the job done, signing a prospect—obviously considered marginal at the time—who would become an all-time Yankees great.

Mattingly was clearly no ordinary 19th-round pick, taken after 492 others had gone before him. He was too small, too slow, and he didn't hit for power. His penchant for hitting the ball the other way, to left or left-center field—a swing developed while playing Wiffle ball in the backyard as a kid to avoid a big tree in "right field"—just wasn't attractive to a lot of people.

Those people were wrong.

* * *

Mattingly didn't care how much he was getting paid. He was playing a game he loved every day and didn't have to worry about anything else. He got married young, so the money mattered. But his drive was all about climbing the ladder.

"I never really thought about [money]. I just wanted to go to the next level every year," he said. "I played A-Ball, and I wanted to go to Double A. When I played in Double A, I wanted to go to Triple A in the next year.

"I remember in '81, I think it was in Nashville, I had a pretty good year. It was funny because Yogi [Berra] was around and [Joe] Pepitone was around—they sent the coaches around to the minor leagues. Then I heard rumblings about going to the big leagues from there. They'll call you up at the end of the year. I thought, *God, I'm not ready for that. I haven't played Triple A yet.*"

Before that, an 18-year-old Mattingly reported to Oneonta, New York, for the half-season league, and in 53 games he batted .349 with three homers and 31 RBIs. He had 30 walks and struck out just six times in 166 at-bats.

"I loved Legion baseball in the summer because you played pretty much every night," he said. "In high school you played once a week or twice a week, and it felt like you practiced all the time in between. And I remember being in Oneonta thinking, *Man, I love this. It's like Legion, but I'm getting paid.* $238 every two weeks. It was cool. At least, I thought it was.

"I never really thought about the next step. I just thought, *Okay, I'm here playing and I'm going to hit.*"

Mattingly married Kim Sexton that September and was on his way to Greensboro, North Carolina, where Bob Schaefer—a former minor league infielder who would become a long-time baseball man and Mattingly's friend—inherited this raw, hardworking talent.

It was there that the Yankees brass suggested Mattingly, who actually threw right-handed as a little boy and was ambidextrous, move to second base. After all, there were guys like Steve Balboni, Marshall Brant, and Todd Demeter ahead of him on the organizational depth chart at first base, and the Yankees were always signing bigger-name free agent first basemen.

The experiment never got off the ground. Sure, Mattingly was at second base for the resumption of the Pine Tar Game, and he played third against Seattle in 1986 and even started a 5-4-3 double play when the ball was hit to him, but he did that crazy stuff *left*-handed.

"It was my first year managing in the minor leagues. Jack Butterfield hired me to manage Greensboro," said Schaefer, who almost two decades later wound up as the Dodgers bench coach, joining the staff when Mattingly, hired to be the hitting coach, suggested Joe Torre give Schaefer a call.

"Don Mattingly was one of the players on the team, along with Greg Gagne. [Mattingly] was a left fielder then. Todd Demeter was our first baseman, a high draft choice, about 6'5"—and Donnie was the left fielder. I guess the year before, the half-year [season], he was a DH most of the time, but we put him in left field. Ken Berry, the outfield coach, did a really good job with him defensively."

But it wasn't the fielding that stood out in Schaefer's mind.

"You could see from the beginning that he just had a knack for being a really good hitter," Schaefer said. "His concentration level for an 18-, 19-year-old kid was exceptional. He hit the ball basically to left field/left-center field, kind of like an opposite-field hitter. He drove the ball the other way. He very rarely pulled the ball, but he was a great RBI guy.

"He batted third. Otis Nixon batted leadoff, and if you go back and look at the stats, I think [Nixon] scored more than 100 runs and Donnie knocked him in probably 80 percent of the time."

Mattingly won the batting title at Greensboro with a .358 average and drove in 105 runs but still hit just nine homers. He walked 59 times and struck out just 33 times, carrying the team to the South Atlantic League title.

"He was like Carl Yastrzemski in 1967," Schaefer once said. "If we needed a single, he singled. A double, he doubled. Two runs, he knocked them in. He locked himself in for a two-week period that was almost scary."

But you have to remember that these were the George Steinbrenner Yankees. Nine homers? For a left-handed bat in Yankees Stadium? And he had Balboni, Brant, and Demeter ahead of him.

Balboni played in a total of 295 games in two stints as a Yankee, but he did most of his damage in Kansas City. Brant was one of the great minor-league sluggers, the classic Four-A player who appeared in eight big league games, three of them with the Yankees. Demeter, the son of major leaguer Don Demeter, never made it to the majors after getting a $208,000 signing bonus as a second-round pick in the 1979 draft.

You *know* what happened to Mattingly.

"You could see that he had exceptional ability, but he was a [low] draft choice, so he wasn't a high-profile guy," Schaefer said. "He just made himself a baseball player. He took everything seriously—great concentration, great work ethic.

"I remember one day he was taking a whole bunch of swings, and I said, 'Donnie, you have to back off a little bit.' He said, 'Oh no, I have to take so many swings.' I said, 'I guess you know yourself. You can do it.' But throughout his whole career he took probably more swings than anybody.

It might have led to some of the problems with his back because he was such a workaholic."

The hard work paid off, but we'll never know what all the extra work did to his back. We can only assume.

"We were a long way from Yankee Stadium when we were in Greensboro. We were in Low A, but what I did see was a guy who stayed on the ball, a guy who had great hand-eye coordination, a guy who had great work ethic—which to me is most important—and a guy who had the concentration skills," Schaefer said. "Hitting is concentration. He would rarely get himself out or have a bad at-bat. He made every at-bat count, but he worked at it.

"He drove the ball hard the other way. His power was to left-center field, but he wasn't a home run hitter. In Greensboro, right field was pretty short but Donnie never got into that pull mode, he just got into hitting the ball hard. Most RBIs are balls hit straight away or the other way—and that's why he was a great RBI guy. If you watch any game, most of the rallies are hits that are straight away or the opposite way."

Mattingly did, of course, learn to pull, but he never lost that backyard ability to go the other way. As Schaefer said, he made himself into a great hitter.

"A star is a guy who has talent and intelligence. Donnie had both," Schaefer said. "He didn't have the talent when he first started. He had the tools to work with, but he made himself a good player. And I think guys who make themselves players like that appreciate the game more. I think they work harder and respect the game a lot more.

"For some guys, everything comes easy to them, and they disrespect the game in some ways by not giving 100 percent all the time. Mattingly is a self-made player. He was drafted low, and not because he was unsignable. He was drafted low because I'm sure a lot of scouts didn't project him to be a major league player because he didn't hit for power, he didn't pull the ball. He wasn't the biggest guy in the world, but he was strong and he got stronger as the years went on."

Mattingly made it through the Yankees system at a time when the young guys were getting dealt away. Willie McGee was with him and then traded. After Mattingly came Fred McGriff, and he was gone. The list is a long one.

"One thing about Donnie—he's one of the young guys of that era who was not traded away when he was at a young age," Schaefer said. "I had Greg Gagne and he was traded away, and Willie McGee, Freddie McGriff—you look at a whole bunch of them. At that time, Steinbrenner wanted guys he knew could play in the big leagues rather than guys he *thought* could play in the big leagues. Look at that era and Mattingly was one of the few guys to stay. When they started bringing up the Jeters, Posadas, and those kind of guys, that's when they really started winning, with homegrown talent."

But *second base*?

"We had him in the instructional league, and at the time Donnie could throw right-handed," Schaefer said. "So one day I got a call from New York and they never projected him to be a left fielder, corner outfielder. At the time I don't think anyone even knew he could play first base.

"They said to me, 'Why don't you try him at second base?' It projects like he might be a hitter who could play *second* base. It didn't look like he was going to have much power.

"He really wasn't too bad, but in my experience the best hitters always hit the ball the other way and learned how to pull the ball. That was kind of nixed after a few tries—not that he wouldn't have been able to do it. He could, but there was no need to do it. I remember Mickey Vernon saying, 'Why would we want to do this to this guy?'

"He just worked out. He could have been acceptable there. I moved him back to the outfield and eventually moved him back to first base. He made himself a player. He made himself a good left fielder. Then, of course, he made himself a tremendous first baseman."

And those power numbers would come—but only after Mattingly got to Yankee Stadium and the big leagues.

"They said he couldn't play first base. They said [he] couldn't pull the ball," Yogi Berra said in Mattingly's *Yankeeography* on the YES Network. "They said, 'No, he doesn't have enough pop to do it.' I said, 'Gosh, he's only 18, 19 years old. He'll learn to pull once he sees the Stadium.'"

* * *

In 1981, Mattingly moved on to Nashville, where he would hit .314 and drive in 98 runs—splitting his time between the outfield and first base. After stroking 32 doubles at Greensboro, he led the Southern League with 35 in '81. But he hit just seven homers and had a minor league personal-worst 55 strikeouts.

The Nashville Sounds, with future Most Valuable Players Mattingly and Willie McGee (strangely, both the same season, 1985, after McGee was traded to St. Louis), lost to the Orlando Twins in the league championship series.

"When Mattingly was playing in the minor leagues, probably Double A ball (Nashville), Dick Gernert was a professional scout and had that league," said Tom Grieve, the Rangers farm director at the time and later Texas' general manager. "When we would have organizational meetings, probably back-to-back years, Dick Gernert said, 'If you're ever dealing with the Yankees, they probably won't trade him because I'm sure they like him too, but the best hitter I've seen in the minor leagues is Don Mattingly.'

"And so, whoever the general manager was—Eddie Robinson or Joe Klein—I'm sure that every time they talked to the Yankees and there was any kind of a significant discussion, Mattingly was someone they asked for. I'm sure every team did."

In 1982, Mattingly moved on to Columbus, where, still primarily an outfielder, he hit .315 with 10 homers and 75 RBIs in 130 games. He struck out just 24 times in 476 at-bats that season.

Broadcaster Rick Rizzs called the Columbus games that year and was working for the Mariners when Mattingly's career ended in Seattle.

"Everything about the guy told you that he was going to be something special," Rizzs said, looking back almost three decades.

"I just saw a talented, quiet kid who was such a good hitter at a very early stage in his career," Rizzs said. "In 1981 we won the Governor's Cup, and Donnie was playing first base in Nashville. When he came up to the Clippers the following year, he was an outfielder—he played 80 or 90 games in the outfield—because at the time the Clippers had two talented first basemen, Marshall Brant and Steve Balboni.

"Mattingly and Balboni were coming up around the same time, but Balboni had the first shot at being the first baseman up in New York. But you could just see in 1982 that [Mattingly] had the ability to hit a baseball, and he had that ability to use the entire field.

"That's what I saw in Don Mattingly—a very talented guy. If you tried to pitch him the other way, he would hit the ball the other way into left field or to left-center field and *drive* the ball. Then you'd make a mistake middle-in and Donnie could pull the ball to right field and hit the ball a long way."

Mattingly's goal that year was clear—get to the next level. That call came late in the season, and he "couldn't believe" the feeling he had the first time he walked onto the field at Yankee Stadium.

He would return to Columbus, though, in 1983 after starting the season in the Bronx playing for Billy Martin. The second stay in the minors, which lasted 43 games, would be his last.

"You knew that he had everything that a big league team wanted in a major league player," Rizzs said. "He was just this quiet kid from Evansville, Indiana, who loved the game of baseball—and it showed. He was polite, he was courteous, and he would never turn me down for an interview.

"Donnie was always, first and foremost, a friend, because when you're in the minor leagues broadcasting, you're with these guys every day, just like when you're in the big leagues. But you're much closer with the players in the minor leagues than you are in the major leagues. And Donnie was just a great kid, very friendly, who loved the game of baseball and it really showed.

"There was no question in my mind that he was going to be an outstanding hitter. How good he was going to be I didn't realize until he actually got to the big leagues. And for four years, he was Lou Gehrig. He was an even better person than he was a ballplayer, and he was a great ballplayer."

Rizzs spotted the leadership qualities that would eventually lead to Mattingly becoming the Yankees captain.

"There was no question about that," Rizzs said. "You could tell that Donnie was a leader and that he was going to do that at the next level, because of the situation that he was put into. The Yankees asked him to go out there and play the outfield in Triple A in 1982, but he was a first baseman. But he went out there and he did it. And he worked hard at it. He said, 'Okay, if you want me to play the outfield.' I'm sure he said this in his own mind, *I'm going to be the best outfielder that I can be*, and he went out there and he did it and he was a good outfielder.

"He had those great hands. But once he moved over to first base, you could see he was a natural there, even in the few games that he played at first base in 1982—the way that he moved, the way that he covered the bag, the way that he went after a ground ball, the way that he fielded. He had those soft hands, and the way that he could pick the ball out of the dirt, you just went, 'Wow, this guy is going to be great at this position.'

"He had a way of getting along with everybody. He never had a bad word to say about anybody. He just soaked it all in. Frank Verdi was a veteran manager at the time, and Donnie learned a lot from Frank. We had Joe Pepitone that year as one of our hitting coaches. Donnie just wanted to learn the game of baseball. He did what he had to do to get to the big leagues. He worked hard at it, and it's no surprise to me that he became one of the best players in the history of the Yankees."

And Mattingly also had to survive the parade of young players who entered and left the organization.

"I was with the Clippers for two years, and it seemed like every year we had 100 transactions or more—guys going up and down," Rizzs said.

"Watching these guys go up and down, up and down, up and down all year, in the back of your mind you knew that if somebody went up you'd see them back in a week or two. Except with Donnie. Donnie played the entire year with us, and when he went up in September, I knew he wasn't coming back. I just knew once he got up there and had a chance to take over at first base that he wasn't coming back again, because he had nothing to prove at Triple A."

But he did come back, and this time he got to play more first base.

"He was just graceful around that bag," Rizzs said. "He had great hands, he could field a ground ball, he got his uniform dirty. It's no shock that down the road he was named captain of the ballclub because of the way he played, the way he took over a leadership role."

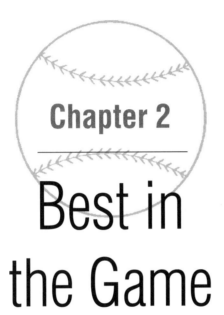

Chapter 2

Best in the Game

"Donnie was a guy who had the reputation that he would play hurt. If he had something wrong with him he would just tape it up and go. He's the type of guy…who would say, 'Wrap it up real hard. I'm still playing.' He would have demanded to play, more than likely."

—Marty Barrett

Mattingly got the first of his 2,153 career regular season hits on October 1, 1982, in the eleventh inning of a game against the Red Sox at Yankee Stadium—a single to right off Steve Crawford in Mattingly's third at-bat in the major leagues. He would finish that month 2-for-12, with a pair of singles and the first of his 1,099 career regular season RBIs.

He recalled his first at-bat. "[Milwaukee's] Jim Slaton," Mattingly remembers. "A nothing fastball right over the plate and I popped it up. I just know I should have crushed it."

Mattingly was 2-for-7 with a pair of RBIs in April 1983 and was sent back to Triple A, the owner of four hits in 19 major league at-bats.

Mattingly went down to Columbus, hit .340 with eight homers in 43 games, and that was that. He returned to the Bronx.

"George Steinbrenner called a dear friend of all of ours, Bobby Murcer, in the office and he said, 'Bobby, you're going to retire tomorrow,'" said former Yankees reliever George Frazier. "And [Murcer] said, 'Well, why?' Steinbrenner said, 'Well, I'm going to give you a three-year contract.

You're going to become a TV announcer, and I'm bringing up a kid named Mattingly who's going to take your place on the ballclub.'

"So one guy who I think was a tremendous player was replaced by another guy who is just a tremendous player and a tremendous person. It's kind of a funny story how George broke it to Bobby Murcer how his career was over.

"But [Murcer] went to the broadcast booth and got a three-year extension, like George normally did, and he got more money."

Mattingly, on the other hand, wound up playing in 91 games with a 1983 Yankees team that finished 91–71 and went nowhere but home. Billy Martin was the manager and he was gone after the season, replaced by Yogi Berra.

"On the first day of camp, Yogi said, 'You're my swing man,'" Mattingly said. "I said, 'If you get me in there, you're not going to be able to get me out.'"

Mattingly was right.

* * *

Butch Wynegar was traded to the Yankees from the Twins during the 1982 season. In September of that year, Don Mattingly was called up from the minor leagues.

For Wynegar, who had already been in the major leagues since 1976, the arrival of Mattingly meant a new friend in his life. A close friend.

He also remembers noticing something—the kid could play.

"There was nothing that told me this kid couldn't play at the major league level," said Wynegar, who today works for the Yankees as a Triple A batting coach. "The way he went about his business, the way he went about his work in the cage, his batting practice—you could tell the kid had a desire to be good.

People keep talking about work ethic. Wynegar admired it in Mattingly from day one and wishes young players coming along today could be just like Donnie.

"The things I look for nowadays are tremendous work ethic and a great makeup," Wynegar said.

Wynegar remained a Yankee until 1986, and he was there for three seasons in which Mattingly bat .343, .324, and .352; hit 89 homers; drove in 368 runs; and also smacked 145 doubles. Mattingly won the batting title in 1984 and was named the American League Most Valuable Player in 1985.

"After he became a superstar type of player, in the years he put together, the more money he made, he never changed. And that's what I really admired about him, that we could remain good friends and continue to play cards," Wynegar said. "He never changed his personality.

"I tell the kids nowadays, Donnie was the one guy who stayed humble. I never saw him deny an autograph request—he was just a great makeup-type guy."

And he was a perfectionist.

"I remember a day—and I don't even remember what year it was, '84, maybe '85," Wynegar said with a smile. "He had gotten three hits the night before off Bruce Hurst, while playing Boston. And Bruce was a tough pitcher at that time. Three line-drive hits the night before and the next day I came out for batting practice and Donnie's over with a bucket of balls and a net, hitting one after another, all by himself.

"I walk over to him—this was in late August so it was pretty warm—and he's got sweat just dripping off him. I think he was hitting something like .350 at the time. He was leading the league in hitting. I said, 'Donnie, what are you doing? You just got three knocks last night against Hurst.' He looked at me and said, 'I just…I just feel…I can't feel this…I'm trying to feel this one thing.'

"He couldn't really explain it to me, but it was a feel that he was trying to get. And that was Donnie. He was hitting like .340, .350, and he was trying to find something to hit .360. And I know if he was hitting .360, he would have been doing something to hit .370. I looked at him and I just patted him on the back and said, 'Good luck,' and I walked away.

"He had that kind of work ethic, and I use that kind of example working with kids in the minor leagues. A guy of his nature, of his stature can do that, same as Alex Rodriguez. Watching Rodriguez hit—guys like him can work. I watched [Albert] Pujols when I was in the National League, walking out of the cage with the sweat just pouring off of him. If guys like that can work, there's no reason these young kids can't work. That's just the way Donnie was, and I put Donnie in that class."

It's a very special class.

"It was like when I played for Minnesota and watched Rod Carew hit every day," Wynegar said. "I think, after a while, you almost took it for granted, but you knew when he walked to the plate something special was going to happen. You expected it.

"Donnie's back kind of cut short what he could have done. I used to sit there and watch Donnie, and now I kick myself in the butt for not picking his brain more about hitting. Now as a coach, having coached for the number of years I have, like all coaches I say, 'I wish I would have known then what I think I know now. I could have helped myself more.' I should have picked Donnie's brain more, but instead I used to sit there and watch him and say, 'What is he doing that I'm *not* doing? Is he just blessed with more than me, or he is he doing something special?' And looking back now I can see exactly what he was doing at that time. I just didn't know it then.

"The guy was special. And like I tell kids today, 'If you shake hands with Donnie and you look at him when you meet him, you're going to think, *That's Don Mattingly?* He's not a big, imposing guy. When you shake hands with him, though, you can feel just by his handshake strength that he did something with his hands for a living.

"Donnie used to tell me hitting's from there to there, from the fingertips to the elbow. . . . I used that example a lot with kids, too. Donnie was strong, had good hands. [His swing was] quick, short, compact, everything we teach today in hitting."

Wynegar was asked if he thought Mattingly was just trying to prove people wrong—the ones who said he wasn't big enough, strong enough, or fast enough to be a real factor. Wynegar said if Mattingly was, "We never talked about it." But the ex-catcher admits it may have been a factor.

"Donnie was just instilled with work ethic, and that's something we battle nowadays. Can you instill work ethic in a kid in the minor leagues? Is he born with it? Is he raised with work ethic? I talk to my farm director and ask, 'What about makeup? Why don't we have a grade for that?'

"You can change a kid to a certain point, get him to work a little harder and understand what it means, but guys like Donnie…they were instilled with it from childhood.

"Maybe deep in Donnie's mind he didn't think he was as good as he was and because his work ethic was so good he pushed himself. I love guys who push themselves, who want to go to the cage, who want to do things, who come get you and say, 'Let's work on this, work on that.' And looking back, that's the way I see Donnie."

Wynegar said being around Mattingly was even more special because he was so consistent.

"With guys like Donnie and Dave Winfield and A-Rod, you know what you're going to get every day when you come to the ballpark," he said. "I tell young guys with talent, 'You need to break through to another level with hard work. If those guys can do it, why can't you?' That's why I had so much appreciation for Donnie."

* * *

Mattingly's 1984 batting title was the start of a marvelous six-year run that had many people thinking he was the best player in baseball.

"I think he's the greatest single player in our game," Hall of Fame manager Sparky Anderson told the *New York Times* in 1988. George Brett, quoted in the same piece, said, "If he isn't the best, I'd like to know who is." Hall of Fame manager Earl Weaver said, "I've never seen anyone like him."

In 1985 at the age of 24, Mattingly hit .324 with 35 homers and 145 RBIs. The Yankees won 97 games but didn't make the playoffs. At the time there was no wild card, so only the two division winners advanced. The Royals won the West with 91 wins, and the Yankees were 7–5 against Kansas City. The Yankees played golf; the Royals won their first and only World Series to date.

The same fate came to the Yankees in 1986. Mattingly, despite leading the league with 238 hits, just missed the batting title, finishing .352—.005 points behind future teammate Wade Boggs. Mattingly, who was never supposed to hit with power, hit 31 homers and drove in 113 runs. The Yankees won 90 games but again stayed home. Mattingly was hitting like crazy, but the Yankees couldn't get over the hump.

"It's tough when you have a club that can win and you're losing," Mattingly told the *New York Times*. "A lot of people make a big deal out of it, but to me it's not that big a deal. Two or three of those years we had the second- or third-best record in baseball, and someone [in the other division] with 10 less wins got in the playoffs."

In 1987, Mattingly hit .327 with 30 homers and 115 RBIs. He also homered in eight straight games, smacking 10 overall during the run, and also hit all six of his career grand slams in that season. In the '88 season he averaged .311 with 18 home runs and 88 RBIs, and he batted .303 with 23 homers and 113 RBIs in 1989.

Mattingly credits former teammate, coach, and manager Lou Piniella with the power stroke.

"For me, Lou was the guy who really had me starting to hit for power," Mattingly said. "As much as anything, he just kind of showed me how the swing worked, which really helped me for teaching too. He taught me the mechanics, the chain reaction—when you do this, it causes this. From him I learned so much about how the swing works.

"Lou would come back to you and say, 'You know, I was in your stance last night and I see right here, you've got to do this,' and it always made sense to me. I was always able to take it and use it. He would do it himself and knew exactly what move I was making, what I was doing right and wrong, and he could suggest a small change and make a big difference. He had me shifting my weight, and he taught me how to stay back, which came from Charlie Lau. He taught me to use my bottom hand more because that's what creates all the power. I had been using my top hand."

* * *

Don Mattingly won the American League batting title in 1984, beating out teammate Dave Winfield. He almost won it in 1986 but narrowly lost to Boston's Wade Boggs. Both races were exciting down the stretch—one a New York Civil War of sorts between two players on the same team, the other between hitters from baseball's hottest rivals.

Mattingly had arrived in 1984—playing a first full season for the ages. The team wasn't in contention for the postseason, but Mattingly and Winfield ran a race that came down to the very end of the season.

And as the summer went on, the New York tabloids pitted the two against each other as rivals. The fans sided with Mattingly over Winfield, the big-money guy who would later be labeled "Mr. May" by his boss.

Mattingly won the race on the final day.

"I was just hitting. I was simply hitting," Mattingly said. "It was my first full year. I had just arrived in the big leagues and I was hitting .330. I was figuring it out—hitting some homers, driving in runs. I was having a *good* year—for a kid who hadn't hit more than eight anywhere he'd been and I had 15, and I kept hitting homers and driving in runs. And I was in the *big leagues* and doing it."

Winfield's 1984 batting average marked a career high and only his third year better than .300 in 11 major league seasons to that point. "It was just two guys [who] were diligent to their trade," Winfield said in the YES Network's Mattingly *Yankeeography*. "That's what attracted people to the stadium because we were out of [the pennant race]."

"I think it's kind of neat, the two of us fighting for the title," Mattingly said in 1984. "Just think, we don't have to check the papers to see which one is ahead, not as if it was Dave and, say, Kent Hrbek. I like it this way."

As he did with most things baseball, Mattingly was having fun with it. After all, it was his first full season in the major leagues.

"Obviously, I wanted to win the batting title, too," he said. "I'm sure Winny wanted to win it, I wanted to win it. That's just the way people are. I had fun because when I look back on it, he had the bad road, I had the good road.

"I was a young kid in New York, and you know how New York works, or any big city—I'm the young kid, coming up, making no money, winning the batting title. And he was a free agent, made tons of money, and had a big ol' contract. He's Dave Winfield, the Boss is on him. I was this young, fresh face that just came and played. [Winfield] had to deal with all the other stuff.

"We didn't really talk about it," Mattingly continued. "We just went out and played. I was always totally respectful of him and what he did. I thought he was a great player. We were teammates trying to win games. We weren't that good that year, but still, he was on my side.

"We were just both hitting. But looking back, he had all the pressure. I was a young kid. If it happened 10 years later and it was Jeter, it would probably have been the same way. Everybody roots for the underdog. Everybody wants to see the underdog win. [Winfield's] relationship with Mr. Steinbrenner…they had some bitterness going on. I didn't understand all that, and I didn't pay attention to it."

Mattingly finished with 207 hits and a .343 batting average, and the home run stroke finally appeared. He hit 23 while driving in 110 runs. Winfield batted .340 with 19 homers and 100 runs batted in.

Mattingly became the first Yankees batting champion since Mickey Mantle won the Triple Crown in 1956.

The Yankees finished 87–75 in 1984, which translated to third place in the American League East.

Steinbrenner, always willing to do media battle with the Mets, said earlier that year, "You can talk all you want about [Darryl] Strawberry. I'll take Mattingly. He's the best young talent in baseball today…he'll be the batting champion in three years."

The Boss was off—by a lot. But 1984 would mark Mattingly's only major league batting title.

In 1986, the Red Sox won the AL East, but the batting race came down to the final weekend of the season—four games in Boston.

Wade Boggs, at .357 after going 1-for-4 in the previous series finale against Baltimore, had a hamstring tear and, with the playoffs coming up for the Red Sox, sat on the bench and watched. Mattingly, at .350 coming in, was going to go it alone.

Most baseball fans are familiar with the tale of Ted Williams in 1941, when Teddy Ballgame could have sat in a last-day double-header and finished at .400. Instead he played both games, went 6-for-8, and finished at .406. It was what Boston fans expected of Boggs in the final series. When he didn't play, there were questions. A New York tabloid blared the headline "Chickened Out," a reference to Boggs' daily pregame diet of chicken.

Mattingly told Boggs at the time, "If you read one quote that even hints at my questioning you, then it's been twisted or it's a fabrication. You know me. We're friends. If I were you, if I were hurting and had the playoffs to think about, then I'd do the same thing. The team comes first."

Looking backing on it now, Mattingly's feelings haven't changed.

"Would I have sat? He was hurt," Mattingly said. "He had a hamstring injury. If you're hurt, and you have the playoffs coming, you'd sit. If I had a bad hammy, I would want to be totally healthy when those playoffs started.

"I played winter ball in Puerto Rico in '83 and won the batting title over there. They sat me late. We were way back, and my team wanted me to win the batting title. I think I hit .367 and Randy Ready might have hit .362. Tony Gwynn was hitting way up there, too. And you know what? It was late in that season, and I was tired. So I didn't play, and I won the title. But it didn't feel that good. I told myself after that [experience] that I would never do that again. I look back and I'm kind of embarrassed that I didn't play those games. But an injury is something different."

Boggs remembers his situation differently.

"When we found out that we were going to the playoffs...I took a lot of flak for that weekend," Boggs said. "Everybody said, 'Why can't you play?'...and I said, 'I've got a hole in my hamstring and I've got to get it ready for the postseason,' and that it was basically doctor's orders, from Dr. [Arthur] Pappas. He said, 'If you play this weekend you've got a good chance of blowing out your hamstring and not playing in the postseason.'

"This was the first time that I had gone to the postseason.... Naturally, I would have loved to have been out there and gone about it, but the injury kept me off the field."

Boggs and Mattingly became closer when Boggs joined the Yankees in 1993, and the final weekend of the 1986 season came up in conversation one day.

"We had talked about that after I went to New York...and [Mattingly] reiterated the same thing, saying, 'If the shoe was on the other foot, I would have done the same thing,'" Boggs said. "It wasn't even apples to oranges for me to be compared to Ted Williams sitting out. I didn't do that in Triple A when I lost a batting title; I could have sat out when Dave Engle beat me back then. But I knew the Ted Williams story and read his book.

"[Pawtucket manager] Joe Morgan asked me if I wanted to hit. I said, 'Yeah, I'm not going to win the batting title like *that*.' So it was apples to oranges. In a perfect world, I wish I would have been 100 percent, not on the cusp of blowing out a hamstring. Dr. Pappas could have stuck his whole thumb into my hamstring—that's how deep the tear was. He said, 'You're going to need these five days to let it get well.' And even then I didn't really know if it was going to be 60, 70 percent when we started playing the Angels.

"That was part of the hype...that followed us around that year. I mean, if it had been me and George Brett or me and Rod Carew, it wouldn't have been that big of a deal. But having the New York writers and the Boston writers go back and forth and having Dr. Pappas come out in the paper and say, 'Yeah, he's got a torn hamstring.' It wasn't like I was ducking Don Mattingly. That wasn't the issue at all."

Mattingly went 2-for-4 in the opener of the four-game series to stay at .350. He then went 3-for-5 in Game 2 to go to .352. A 1-for-5 on Saturday left him at .351, which meant he needed to go 6-for-6 Sunday to win the batting title.

Lou Piniella, knowing the long odds that this crazy thing could ever happen, batted Mattingly leadoff in the final game, and Mattingly led the game off with a home run off Jeff Sellers. That got people interested and spawned some stories about Boggs that are probably fables.

"Bruce Hurst told me that after that [homer], Boggsie went up and started to warm up," said Mike Pagliarulo, the Yankees third baseman at the time. "I mean, my God. He shouldn't have played—if it would have hurt the team he wouldn't have done it, no way."

According to Marty Barrett, Boggs' teammate, "Boggs started warming up, like, *I better get ready, I might have to go get a hit.* It was really kind of funny watching that and halfway thinking, *Man, this guy might be able to do it.*

"Donnie was a guy who had the reputation that he would play hurt. If he had something wrong with him, he would just tape it up and go. He's the type of guy...who would say, 'Wrap it up real hard. I'm still playing.' He would have demanded to play, more than likely."

Boggs has no recollection of getting up for warm-ups or even saying anything about it. At least, not seriously.

"You know me, and you've covered me enough to [believe my] guarantee that I said it in jest," Boggs told this author. "There was no way I was going to go in that Sunday game. Mac [Red Sox manager John McNamara] wouldn't have let me go in. He would have said, 'You're going to lose the batting title, and we're going to the playoffs.' That would have been the scenario. I wouldn't have gone in the game to jeopardize not playing in the playoffs."

Besides, Boggs said, "He needed six hits. In order to get six hits.... I mean, he could have gone 5-for-5 very easily. But having six at-bats in a game was not going to be. If he would have gone 6-for-6, it wouldn't have said much about our pitching staff."

Teammate Jim Rice agreed. "Our pitchers had something in the backs of their minds, too, [with] both guys going for the batting title," Rice said. "So what you do is you walk him—and get the batting title for our guy."

Mattingly made out his second time up and was done, but then he doubled his third trip, his 53rd double of the season, breaking Lou Gehrig's Yankees record. He asked for the ball, which was sent over to the Yankees dugout. Piniella got the ball and was laughing as he faked tossing it into the crowd.

Mattingly finished 2-for-5 with three RBIs and .352 for the year, just shy of Boggs' mark. It was something he felt would rightfully belong to Boggs for some time.

"I said over the winter that until Wade retires, to even think about a batting title, you have to think .350," Mattingly said at the time. "Well, I got close. That's an accomplishment. I just hope he's healthy for the playoffs, because he plays hard every day. I feel like we're the same in a lot of ways."

Barrett has not forgotten the determination in Mattingly that last day.

"When he hit that ball deep, he screamed. He hit it and went, 'Yahhhhhhhhhhh,'" Barrett remembered. "I thought, *What the heck was that?* I thought, *Man, this guy is crazy, but he's going to do this, maybe.*"

* * *

It really is hard to decide which Mattingly season was better—1985 or 1986.

He was the Most Valuable Player in '85, hitting 35 homers and driving in 145 runs with a slugging percentage of .567 and an OPS of .939. He led the league with 370 total bases and had a .371 on-base percentage.

The next year featured the batting race with Boggs, and Mattingly actually raised some of his other numbers as well as adding 28 points to his batting average. He dropped from 35 homers and 145 RBIs to 31 and 113 but went from 211 to 238 in hits, .567 to .573 in slugging, 48 doubles to 53, .939 to .967 in OPS, and .371 to .394 in on-base percentage. The hits and doubles both set Yankees records.

What's most staggering of all is that he had all that production and only 76 strikeouts combined during the two seasons.

* * *

Back in April 1986, Mattingly, Wade Boggs, and Ted Williams sat down in a Clearwater, Florida, restaurant with Peter Gammons of *Sports Illustrated*. The get-together became part of the magazine's "Baseball 1986, Here Come the Hitters" season preview issue, and Gammons got the game's two best young hitters together with the man many think is the greatest hitter of all time.

The interview covered a variety of topics, but much of it had Ted arguing with the approach of the modern guys. Toward the end, Boggs told Williams, "Ask Don the question you asked me about the bat burning."

Earlier, on the ride over from Winter Haven where Williams and Boggs were together at Red Sox camp, Williams said to Boggs, "Have you ever smelled the smoke from the wood of your bat burning?" To which Boggs replied, "What?"

"The smell of the smoke from the wood burning," Williams repeated.

"What are you talking about, Ted? I don't understand."

"Five or six times, hitting against a guy with good stuff, I swung hard and—*oomph*—just fouled it back. Really hit it hard. And I smelled the wood of the bat burning. It must have been that the seams hit the bat just right and the friction caused it to burn, but it happened five or six times."

Boggs shook his head and said, "Awesome."

Later, when three left-handed hitters who combined for 7,817 hits and a .327 lifetime batting average were sitting together, Williams asked Mattingly, "Have you ever smelled the smoke from the wood burning."

Mattingly answered, "I've had it happen. Yeah. Twice, for sure. All of a sudden, I smelled a real big burn, and at the same time I was thinking, *I just missed that one.* Two or three times. I've never told that to anyone, because I didn't think anyone would believe me. I think one of the bat burns came off of [Edwin] Nunez."

Said Boggs, "That's the damnedest thing I've ever heard. I thought I'd heard everything about hitting, but that's unbelievable. Amazing."

* * *

Willie, Mickey, and the Duke. You know all about the intra-city war that went on when the three Hall of Famers patrolled center field for the Giants, Yankees, and Dodgers, respectively. If you rooted for one of those teams, your guy was Willie Mays, Mickey Mantle, or Duke Snider.

Three decades later, a similar controversy brewed in the Big Apple. Don Mattingly and Keith Hernandez were New York's two high-profile first basemen.

"That was always the battle in New York—who was better," broadcaster Tim McCarver said recently. "Oh, it was unbelievable. [They were] two guys who were maybe the best fielding first basemen in the history of the game."

Hernandez is regarded by many as the best defensively at the position. But Mattingly is not far behind. McCarver believes Hernandez had the stronger arm, giving him the edge.

"I agree with Timmy on that," said fellow broadcaster Gary Thorne, who also worked for the Mets at the time. "It is very hard to judge Keith— and I think it's hard to judge any defensive player—unless you do it on a day-by-day basis. When you saw Keith play every day, you realized the little things he did. Nobody I have ever seen, not before and not now, plays the bunt at first base the way he did. He made plays at third base to get outs on attempted sacrifices like no other first baseman I have ever seen."

"I know this—if you had to pick two names, [Hernandez and Mattingly] are two of the first that would come up," said longtime coach Jackie Moore. "I'm sure there have been some guys who have been close, but for all-around players I don't know if you could pick any better than [those two]."

Buck Showalter added, "[Mattingly was] pretty special. Donnie impacted the game defensively, too, and that's a thing a lot of people didn't realize. You find a lot of guys who can catch a ground ball and scoop a low throw. But Donnie was a fearless thrower. You think about the great first basemen, [and] Keith and Donnie both were fearless throwers. They'd throw the ball across the diamond, they'd go 3-6-3. I remember Donnie playing on the outfield grass with the bases loaded and a guy hit a one-hop seed to his right. I thought, *What in the world is he going to do with this?* and he just turned and threw the ball to second base."

Said Ken Harrelson, a Yankees broadcaster in 1987 and '88, "I guess in that time you could throw a blanket over him and Keith Hernandez... they were both terrific. But nobody was better than Mattingly at first base."

Both could hit—really hit—but Mattingly was the more prolific of the two.

"You talk about Mattingly's offense," McCarver said. "I remember when I was working with ABC and he had all the home runs in eight straight games. We were doing a game in Texas. I remember how exciting it was to be around.

"And he was always such a classy guy, the way he carried himself. I didn't know him at the time, but I was always impressed with the way he carried himself and the way he approached the game. [He had a] religious concentration on what he was doing and how he went about his job. And when you play the game a long time, you really learn to appreciate guys like that."

Off the field, these men were as different as night and day. Mattingly was as American as apple pie, the scruffy kid from the Midwest who never got near controversy. Hernandez was...well, let's just say *he wasn't* Don Mattingly off the field.

But they were both great. Hernandez was the 1979 co-MVP in the National League. Mattingly won the award in the AL in 1985. Hernandez won the batting title in '79, while Mattingly won in '84.

Mattingly came up to the Yankees when Hernandez was helping the Cardinals win the 1982 World Series. Then on June 15, 1983—the trade deadline at that time—the Mets shipped pitchers Neil Allen and Rick Ownbey to the Cards for Hernandez. With the Mets ready to show what they had in Dwight Gooden and Darryl Strawberry, Hernandez would become a cornerstone of a Mets team that would win the 1986 World Series and probably should have won more.

So they were together in New York. But in 1983, when Mattingly was a rookie and Hernandez was just getting there, there was no way of knowing what that meant until the following season.

The comparisons between the two players in the next four years are staggering.

Mattingly hit .343, .324, .352, and .327 with 23, 35, 31, and 30 homers and drove in 110, 145, 113, and 115 runs. Hernandez batted .311, .309, .310, and .290. Not a slugger and not playing in a home park with a short right-field porch, Hernandez hit 15, 10, 13, and 18 home runs and totaled 94, 91, 83, and 89 RBIs.

Additionally, each first baseman won his respective league's Gold Glove in each of those four years.

"When you can compare Don Mattingly with Keith Hernandez—when you can compare *anybody* with Keith Hernandez, you've really done something," Thorne said. "I think the throwing arm was the biggest difference.

"Two very good first basemen really dominated the time frame in major league baseball. And when it's happening in New York, there's the annual which-would-you-take-at-each-position battle between the Yankees and Mets that always goes on around town," Thorne continued. "And it was *really* a heightened discussion when those two were playing... and the arguments raged back and forth. You're always after the back page of the tabloids in New York, and those two guys tended to get it a good deal of the time, for what they were doing both offensively and defensively. It was really kind of fun. There was a real war going on with the fans as to which one to pick."

Thorne added, "I think Keith had fun with it. Keith was so focused and directed on the games—the Mets were a winning ballclub at the time and had the '86 World Series championship—that his focus was always on the game. He liked Don. They got along well, from everything I know.

I don't think he viewed it as any kind of a rivalry as such, because for Keith the rivalry was always from within. It was to be the best first baseman in the game while he was playing and maybe the best first baseman ever, and that's what he focused on—not so much on the rivalry. I don't think it bothered him at all. He probably found it fun."

Hernandez, the established leader of those Mets, and Mattingly, arriving as some big names were leaving the Yankees, were the clear leaders of their respective teams.

"[Keith] was a team leader in every sense of the word on and off the field and his play was spectacular offensively and defensively," Thorne said. "He made a big difference on the championship team and the winning that they had there, while Don was on a team that was struggling.

"I think if there was any pressure playing in the city against one another, it had to be on Don—not for anything that the two of them were doing but because of the team's situation. With the Yankees taking it on the head every day because they were being compared to the Mets and the fact that they weren't putting together championships at the time, I think it made it more difficult for Don."

Then there was the ownership. While Mattingly had his battles with George Steinbrenner, can you imagine what might have happened if Hernandez had played for the Boss?

"It would have been great TV," Thorne said. "Keith was not one to hold back on anything. I don't think that would have worked. It either would have [required] Steinbrenner accepting Keith on Keith's terms or just leaving him alone or it wouldn't have worked—they would have come to loggerheads and it would have been public and it wouldn't have been pretty."

* * *

Dale Long was a first baseman for the Pirates in 1956 when, during his best power season in the major leagues and only All-Star season, he homered in eight straight games.

Thirty-one years later, Don Mattingly became the second major leaguer to homer in eight straight games, hitting a record 10 over that span.

The home run streak record is not all Mattingly and Long shared; there's another rather strange connection between the players. While Mattingly was coming through the Yankees farm system, there was a suggestion the Yanks try him as a second baseman—a right-handed-throwing second baseman—since he was an ambidextrous child and because he wasn't expected to hit with any power. The experiment was short-lived, but Mattingly did appear at both second and third base during his career. Long was a left-handed thrower who played catcher in two games for the Cubs in 1958, as another experiment.

But the versatile left-handed hitters didn't have the record to themselves for all that long. Ken Griffey Jr. did it, too, in 1993. Griffey hit 630 career homers before retiring during the 2010 season, whereas Mattingly hit 222 and Long 132.

As it turned out, 1987 was a strange year all around for home runs baseball. Mattingly's future teammate, Matt Nokes, hit 32 of his 136 career homers with the Tigers that year, and Wade Boggs cracked 24, the only season he hit more than 11. Mattingly, just six weeks after his first stay on the disabled list because of back injuries, belted 10 of his 222 career home runs during the streak.

"He was just hitting bombs everywhere," said then-teammate Mike Pagliarulo.

Said Michael Kay, a newspaper reporter covering the team, "We were all mesmerized by it in the press box."

Two of the homers, off Chicago's Joel McKeon and Texas' Charlie Hough, came with the bases loaded—two of Mattingly's six grand slams that season. Mattingly had never hit a grand slam in the major leagues before that season and amazingly never hit one again.

"You challenge Donnie Mattingly when he's swinging the bat [well]? Not a good idea," Pagliarulo said. "These guys were trying to throw that ball in there, throw it by him, and [that's when] he's got you."

It started with a pair of home runs on July 8 at Yankee Stadium, with Juan Berenguer (a solo shot) and Mike Smithson (a three-run blast) of the Twins as the victims.

Then came a solo homer off Richard Dotson of the White Sox on July 9 with the slam off McKeon in game 3. Solo shots off Chicago's Jose DeLeon and Jim Winn followed in games 4 and 5. Then came a trip into the Texas heat, when Mattingly hit a pair in game 6—the grand slam off Hough and a two-run shot off Mitch Williams in a seven-RBI game. In game 7, Paul Kilgus yielded a solo shot. Then Mattingly got Jose Guzman—who would be offered to the Yankees by the Rangers in a deal for Mattingly just a year later—for an opposite-field solo shot on July 18.

"The Streak" came to an end in Texas, where the Yankees lost 20–3 on July 19. Mattingly had *only* a double in that game, setting an American League record with an extra-base hit in 10 straight games. The night after that, playing first base behind a Tommy John complete game at the Metrodome, Mattingly tied a major league record for first basemen with 22 putouts in a nine-inning game.

Don Mattingly's Home Run Streak in the Summer of 1987:

Date	Opponent	Pitcher	Men on Base	W-L
July 8	Twins	Smithson	2	W
July 8	Twins	Berenguer	0	W
July 9	White Sox	Dotson	0	L
July 10	White Sox	McKeon	3	W
July 11	White Sox	DeLeon	0	L
July 12	White Sox	Winn	0	W
July 16	@Rangers	Hough	3	W
July 16	@Rangers	Williams	1	W
July 17	@Rangers	Kilgus	0	W
July 18	@Rangers	Guzman	0	L

Mattingly was 17-for-37 during that summer home run stretch, posting a nifty .459 batting average. During the run, Mattingly drove in 21 runs and amazingly scored only one run that didn't come on a home run.

"At the time he was in that streak, I was swinging the bat as [well] as I was all season," Pagliarulo said. "We never really talked about, 'I'm going to get more hits than you today,' or 'I'm going to do this or that,' but we were hitting home runs every day—both of us. He'd hit one, maybe I'd hit one, but he'd hit another one, he'd keep going, every day. And I'm like, 'You better cut this stuff out, I'll take over now.' And I'd hit a home run and he'd say, 'Oh yeah, watch this,' and he'd hit a home run. I kept thinking, *What the hell's going on?*

"So in Texas, he got up there for his first at-bat and hit a home run. I was thinking, *What the heck?* Then he came in and I said, 'That's enough. I'm putting an end to this. I'm going to hit a home run.' So I went and hit a home run and he goes, 'I'm not done yet,' and he hit another home run to the opposite field. You can't try to hit home runs. I wasn't trying to hit home runs, we were just playing around. I mean, you can't do that—but he was actually doing it. He was actually hitting the ball out."

Pagliarulo hit three homers in the eight games, while Mattingly hit 10!

Clearly, nothing Mattingly did surprised Pagliarulo. "He can hit home runs at Yankee Stadium, and he can hit a lot of them," he said. "If he played there for 20 years, he would have 500. He can hit home runs [there] because he could pull the ball when he wanted to and pull it easy. You throw him inside off the plate and he'll still keep the ball fair."

* * *

Rickey Henderson loved playing with Don Mattingly. Apparently, the feeling was mutual.

Henderson, a future Hall of Famer (who would name Mattingly in his induction speech among his great teammates) and baseball's all-time base stealer, left the Yankees during the season in 1989 under a cloud of suspicion. Rumors were that he had quit on the team, that he had become a distraction through a series of events that began with a spring training claim made after Henderson showed up late for camp. The rumors alleged that the failure of the '88 Yankees could be traced to too much alcohol, both on the team charter and after hours.

The doubts about Henderson seemed to become justified when he went back to Oakland and almost won the Most Valuable Player Award in the second half of the season. In 65 games with the Yankees, he batted .247 with three home runs, 22 RBIs, 25 stolen bases, and 41 runs scored. In Oakland, he hit .294 with nine homers, 35 RBIs, 52 steals, and 72 runs scored.

Some said he became the first player ever to destroy one team in the first half and help win it for another the second. The A's won it all in 1989, and Henderson led the league in steals and runs scored, finishing ninth in the MVP voting.

Mattingly doesn't believe in the negative stuff about Henderson. "I don't really think so," Mattingly said. "People always say Rickey quit, but I don't buy that."

When reminded that Henderson got awfully good awfully quick upon his return to Oakland, Mattingly replied, "Yeah, but that happens, too, with a change of scenery. We were in a bad place, we were not playing well.

"Rickey relied so much on his legs. That was such a big, huge part of his game. You can't sit and judge if Rickey's legs are tight. He knows what he can do and can't do. He took care of himself in that sense and that's why he played so long, I think. You may not like it, but he took care of himself.

"I think we all want to say, 'Go out and play hurt, go out and do it.' You don't care if he plays 10 years instead of 14, you know what I mean? But Rickey took care of himself, as far as his body."

Mattingly notes the pressures put on base stealers to run all the time.

"You think about base stealers like Rickey," he said. "You ask them to play good defense, you ask them to steal bases, you ask them to hit, to get on base. And, really, when he got on base, it's not like when I got on base. When I got on base they weren't throwing over five times. With Rickey it was like, step off, hold, throw over, throw over, go, get on second, and steal a bag for us.

"It's a lot tougher on those guys than people say it is. They have to concentrate on a lot of different areas.… You're asking them to do a lot. The guys who can do more, you ask them to do more."

* * *

Broadcaster Suzyn Waldman was asked recently about the trade talks involving Mattingly after the 1988 season. "There was no way George was ever trading Don Mattingly. It wasn't going to happen."

She's probably right. After all, Mattingly *did* wind up spending his entire career in pinstripes. But the relationship between player and owner—easily the most tempestuous owner in the sport at the time—had deteriorated, and Steinbrenner was actually talking to teams about moving Mattingly.

As he normally did, the Boss had questioned Mattingly in the papers. Mattingly beat him in arbitration and Steinbrenner said, "The monkey is clearly on his back. He has to deliver a championship like Reggie Jackson did. [Mattingly's] like all the rest of them now. He can't play Little Jack Armstrong of Evansville, Indiana, anymore."

He also called Mattingly "the most unproductive .300 hitter in baseball."

Finally, Mattingly, who was not normally vocal, could take no more. "You come here and you play and you get no respect," he said. "They belittle your performance and make you look bad in the media. After they give you the money, it doesn't matter. They can do whatever they want. They think money is respect."

"I remember that quote," Mattingly said recently. "You know what it came after? It came after the home run streak in '87. It came after I won arbitration and [Steinbrenner] had said, 'The farmers in Indiana and the taxicab drivers aren't going to have any respect because all [Mattingly] cares about is money.' I took that and I listened to it and I just took it. *It's*

Don Mattingly's annual salaries:

1983—$35,000	1988—$2,000,000	1993—$3,820,000
1984—$130,000	1989—$2,200,000	1994—$4,020,000
1985—$455,000	1990—$2,500,000	1995—$4,420,000
1986—$1,375,000	1991—$3,420,000	
1987—$1,975,000	1992—$3,620,000	

Source: Baseball-Reference.com (citing various sources)

the Boss, I thought. It didn't really bother me that much. I shouldn't say it didn't bother me, but you can't let that kind of stuff get under your skin.

"That was a period of time for me where that built up, because I took a shot after arbitration. We settled arbitration in the first year right at the deadline. The next year we didn't settle but he called me that night before arbitration because you have to settle by midnight and said, 'Hey, tomorrow, don't be offended. It's just business.' I said okay and I went into arbitration. I never cared, because I thought you couldn't lose in arbitration. When you don't win, you still win.

"So I was not really worried about winning or losing. You go in, they say their thing and I didn't really think it was that bad. Well, I won—I think it was $1.9-something. We settled at $1.3-something the year before. I didn't want to be the guy that broke $2 million, I don't know why, but the Players Association got mad. I won, and then he has the taxi drivers, Little Jack Armstrong, and all this stuff. And I thought, *What happened to, 'This is just business?'* I found out quickly that meant, 'It's a business as long as I win.'"

Mattingly erupted—at least he came as close to erupting as he would ever come. Apparently, Steinbrenner didn't take it well.

Dallas Green had just been named the latest manager in Steinbrenner's managerial carousel. Green called Mattingly and asked him to try to straighten out things with the owner.

"I remember I was packing up the house in New Jersey, heading home for the winter," Mattingly recalled. "Dallas called and asked me, 'Do you want to play?' I said, 'Yeah, I don't want to go anywhere else. But I'm not going to be treated like shit. If he wants to trade me I can't worry about it, but I'm not going to be treated like shit. I *am* a man.'"

"He said, 'Would you be willing to call him? Make the call if you really want to play here.' I said, 'Sure.' So I called him and it kind of got heated. We went back and forth about the respect thing, and I said, 'You can't treat me like that. I come here every year and it's fighting, it's yelling back and forth. It's not respect. Money's not respect. I'm here every year on time. I'm in shape. I'm ready to go. I played every day. I played hurt. You can't treat me that way.'

"At the end of it he basically said, 'Well, good luck to you then.' I hung up and told Kim, 'You know what? We might as well sell this place because we're gone.'"

Rumors of a trade began to swirl. First it was Mattingly and Rick Rhoden for Will Clark, Atlee Hammaker, and Craig Lefferts. The Giants reportedly backed off. But other rumors popped up.

"I heard a little bit about Will Clark...but I don't know if any of that was true," Mattingly said. "I think the reason Steinbrenner was mad was basically because of what I said. And what I said really came from festering through the '87 [streak] and then his comments about the arbitrations. We settled one year and didn't settle the next, but he told me not to take anything personally and then he got mad and threw some quotes out there.

"You let that stuff go because he's the Boss, he's the owner, and then at some point you say, 'Enough.' That's really the reason he was mad at me, because I had basically talked back."

Tom Grieve was the Texas Rangers' general manager back then and recalled his discussions with George. And every time the Rangers would make a proposal, Steinbrenner, who was doing most of the Yankees' talking, would say, "I have better offers from other teams," a sure sign he didn't really want to make a move. The talks went back and forth, but according to Grieve, now a broadcaster for the Rangers, "I don't think it was even close to a deal."

The Yankees asked Grieve for Ruben Sierra, then an up-and-coming star who never quite lived up to his potential. Grieve told Steinbrenner that Sierra and pitcher Bobby Witt were not available. Names floated back and forth, Grieve eventually coming up with a six-for-five proposal that would have sent Charlie Hough, Jose Guzman, Pete O'Brien, Steve Buechele, Curtis Wilkerson, and Bob Brower to New York for Mattingly, Rhoden, Mike Pagliarulo, Al Leiter, and Bobby Meacham.

"I said, 'Man, Texas is going to be a good club,'" Pagliarulo said. "I mean, I didn't want to leave New York—I don't think Donnie did, either—but that was funny. I remember hearing that. And of course I started thinking, *Man, I can't wait. If that ever happened, we'll come back and kick the shit out of New York's team.*"

Added Pagliarulo, "I'm sure that Dallas tried to get Donnie traded. I'm *sure* of it. He tried to trade Winfield, everybody—that was his gig. He wanted to break down the whole club and start all over again. Well, he broke it down and left it broke.

"Moses. That was Dallas. First meeting of the year he said, 'I can't win this thing without you, boys.' Everyone's looking at each other, going, 'What did he just say? He can't win this thing without...*he's* going to win it?'

"At the time it was spring training and the Life section of the *USA TODAY* was open. I looked down and there was a picture in the TV reviews of Charlton Heston. I said, 'There he is—it's Moses.' He didn't like that too much. Moses is going to win the whole thing by himself. He ended up screwing the whole thing up by himself."

But nothing happened to Mattingly in that off-season.

"He said if you mention Jose Guzman, you're in the ballpark—we might keep on talking if he's in the deal," Grieve said.

Guzman, who gave up one of the homers Mattingly hit during his 1987 surge, was 11–13 in the 1988 and would go on to go 43–30 over the rest of his career. It seemed suspect that this right-hander was the guy holding up a deal. Perhaps it was something more than that. Perhaps George was not really thinking of trading Mattingly at all.

"Maybe George was mad. Maybe he wanted to see what he could get," said Grieve, who was also talking to Yankees general manager Bob Quinn. "Maybe he wanted Mattingly to know he was talking to other teams. I don't know what it was—but I knew we would have made a trade for the right players.

"If you're asking me if we were interested in trading for Don Mattingly, the answer is yes. But it kind of died a slow death."

"[Steinbrenner] was never going to trade Don Mattingly," Waldman said. "He would tell me Donnie was like a son to him and he adored [Mattingly's wife] Kim. Kim used to call him all the time—he adored Don Mattingly and George is the kind of person who...didn't like people who rolled over on him. So if Donnie went up and said something or called him, he loved that. You could fight with George—he liked that. He didn't want yes men around him."

On the day of Steinbrenner's death, YES Network's Jack Curry looked back at Mattingly's and Steinbrenner's relationship. "They did have an interesting relationship. Mattingly was a guy who loved to be respected, and I think that's what he was trying to get at that point. He just wanted to know that Steinbrenner was respecting him. He wasn't worried about what was on the paycheck. He just wanted to know that the owner respected him."

So Mattingly stood up to Steinbrenner, and he said that changed their relationship forever.

"From that point on I never had a bit of a problem," Mattingly said. "It's almost like I stood up for myself and he [liked it]. I wasn't going to take it. From that point forward, we'd always see eye to eye."

However, he still hasn't forgotten the way he felt that day after getting off the phone with George.

"He kind of told me, 'Well, good luck,' and slammed the phone down on me," Mattingly told the YES Network the day Steinbrenner died.

But, he added, "From that point we both hashed it out. I stood up for myself and the way I felt about myself. I needed to be treated with some form of respect. From that point forward we never had a problem."

And Mattingly was never traded.

* * *

To Al Leiter as a kid growing up in New Jersey, playing for the Yankees in Yankee Stadium was a dream that came true. And with that dream came the chance to play alongside Don Mattingly.

"For me, it was really special because I grew up 65 miles from the stadium. My most impressionable time was when it was really Donnie Baseball," Leiter said. "He got called up in '82 while I was in high school."

"And then I get drafted by the Yankees, and they did a little dog-and-pony show at the Stadium in '84 [to introduce draftees to the team]. Yogi [Berra] was the manager. I remember meeting Donnie. He couldn't have been nicer. Fast-forward three years later, he was my teammate—and he really was the same; he hadn't changed—a Midwest guy who is the salt of the earth.

"He treated me as he would Ron Guidry or Dave Righetti or Dave Winfield or Rickey Henderson. It was a who's who club back then, and he was always pleasant.

"I was in awe being around him. But once I got to know him, he didn't have that aura of *I'm really good and you're not. I'm the greatest and you're not.*

Did that equanimity make Mattingly successful as a coach and manager? "No doubt about it," said Leiter, who is now a Yankees broadcaster. "From what I saw when he was here with the Yankees—I don't know what he's doing with the Dodgers—[he brings] immediate credibility. He's got the street cred. People know him. They look at his baseball card, so that's established…. Because of how much they make today, players can still be assholes and think *I don't care if you were Donnie Baseball, I'm Joe Willie and I'm making a ton of money.* When they see his behavior and he doesn't come across as a pompous ass, he's able to get these guys to buy into what he's doing and believe in him. And if he was a jerk about it, the guys now with what they make wouldn't listen.

Leiter remembered a moment he shared with Mattingly during the early days of the 1989 season. "I remember coming out onto the field at Yankee Stadium before the game, and he was taping his bat…and he was deep in thought. I said, 'Donnie, what's up?' and he looked at me and kind of shook his head. He said, 'Man, this game's tough.'

"I said, 'Yeah? C'mon, man, you're *Donnie Baseball*, you're *Donnie Baseball*,' and I'm trying to pump him up. I'm like a little shithead, 'You're *Donnie Baseball*.'"

Mattingly started the 1989 season in a 5-for-31 slump, with no home runs and three RBIs. He batted .221 in April and didn't hit his first home run until May 24.

"Winfield was hurt [and missed the entire 1989 season]. Donnie didn't have protection and they were trying to put Claudell [Washington], Gary Ward, and all these other guys behind him, [but] he wasn't getting pitched to. It was somewhere in the middle or the end of April and he wasn't batting Donnie numbers and he was really down.

"He turned to me and said, 'Don't ever forget this. For as good as the good is, the bad's not far behind,'" Leiter remembered.

"Then he went into this whole *bust your ass, work hard* mantra. I always thought about that: *For as good as the good is, the bad's not far behind.* And I think that really encapsulates Donnie. Even when he was Donnie Baseball and he was doing card shows, when he was a rock star, he always had *the bad is right there* [in his mind]" Leiter remembered, pointing over his shoulder. "That's probably what made him that hardworking, blue-collar guy. And it probably worked him out of the game—all the swinging and the hitting he and Pags used to do. They were nonstop, after games, before games. So who knows what that did to his back? [Ron] Guidry used to tell him, 'You have only so many swings.'"

Leiter recalled that the Yankees old guard, led by Guidry and Mattingly, welcomed him into the family. "They embraced me, even though I was a young little punk. Guidry embraced me, and once Gator embraced me, I was allowed to hang with the guys," Leiter said. "It was a blast. I saw Rick Cerone at Joe Namath's golf tournament recently, and we remembered some stories. What a crew, man. It was fun. And I even said, these guys [today] don't have a tenth of the fun we had."

Leiter shook his head when talking about Mattingly. "I referred to him as a rock star—literally," he said. "He liked rock and roll, John Cougar [Mellencamp] and going to concerts. The first time I saw Bruce Springsteen it was Mattingly who invited me to go along. It was me, Pags, Mattingly.... He said, 'Kid, you want to go see Springsteen?' I said, 'Heck yeah.'

"He was a rock star. It was hard for me because as a young player there were so many stars. There were Henderson and Winfield and Gator—who I looked up to as a kid—but it was still Donnie. And he was *quiet.* There was nothing [arrogant] about him. [He had a] quiet, regal presence. Torre [is the same way] but he's kind of grandfatherly.

"You size certain guys up. How he walks, what his shoes look like, how he wears his belt. You just want to be like them."

* * *

Clyde King, who passed away in 2010, was a jack of all trades for George Steinbrenner and one of the truly nice people in the business. He was the manager of the team when Don Mattingly was called up from the minors in September 1982. The Yankees, world champions in 1977 and '78, had gone to the World Series and won the first two games against the Dodgers in '81, the first big strike year, and then lost the next four. Steinbrenner allegedly got into a fight in an elevator in Los Angeles. He apologized to the fans for his team performing unacceptably—especially a year after George Brett and the Royals had finally gotten past New York in the American League Championship Series.

No one knew the four straight losses to the Dodgers in '81 would mark the Yankees' last postseason appearance until 1995, Mattingly's final year as a player.

The 1982 season started the spiral. It was a mess. Bob Lemon, who had led the miracle charge in 1978 and then returned when Gene Michael was fired, was the manager at the start of the season. Michael was slated to return the following year. Lemon, who was in the dugout for the unforgivable Series loss to the Dodgers, was dismissed after just 14 games. Michael was brought back early, but his second stint ended just 86 games later. (Ironically, it was Michael who many credit with saving the franchise in the 1990s through his front-office savvy.) King managed the final 62 games of the season; Mattingly started his career in seven of them, going just 2-for-12.

Billy Martin returned for the 1983 season, but his mercurial relationship with the Boss contributed to yet another dismissal for the embattled manager. Over Mattingly's career, managers came and went, from Martin to Clyde King to Martin to Yogi Berra to Martin to Lou Piniella to Martin to Dallas Green to Bucky Dent to Stump Merrill.

Then, for the last four years of his career, Mattingly played for former minor league teammate Buck Showalter, and the Yankees started to come around. With their owner suspended for two years at the start of the decade, the team began their climb back. Even when George returned in 1993, there was apparently less meddling and more faith in the decision-making of folks like Michael.

Obviously, you look at the managerial list and one name stands out: Billy Martin. If Martin hadn't died, there's no telling how many more times it would have stood out.

"I liked playing for Billy," Mattingly said. "For me, he was the guy who gave me a chance. I made the team in '83. I didn't really expect to make the team, but he took me in '83. Obviously he saw something.

"We had a lot of good players there, and I made the team. Obviously I wasn't playing very much early and he sent me down, but he called me back up and played me. I'll always look at him as the guy who saw something and brought me up.

"Billy was different. I had heard a lot about him, and I remember in '83 that spring training was cake. I thought it was going to be nuts, and it was relaxed. We just had fun. It seemed great, but it shocked me."

Then came the regular season, when Mattingly got to see what everyone else was talking about.

"Then, the opening game was nuts, and I thought, *Wow, there it is*," Mattingly said recently with a smile. "Starting with the first pitch, everything was at the umpires, in their face. It was like, *this one counts*. It was a flip of the switch."

The intensity Martin showed for the game was something that was burning inside Mattingly, too—and had been for a long time.

"To be honest with you, Billy's not one of those managers who you want to see if you're 0-for-4 that night and then run into him in the [hotel] lobby, because I think he took it personally and felt that you really didn't want to get a hit for him that night," Mattingly laughed.

"That's how he managed. That's who he was and that's just the way it was. But it's not so bad as a player if you think, *You know what? I'm just as mad at myself for not getting hits*. If you have that mentality, what did it matter?

"I did everything I could do to get a hit, and I was pissed off at myself for not getting a hit. Billy got mad, but what could I do?"

And in the dugout?

"I didn't pay much attention, honestly," Mattingly said. "He'd yell at the umps and get pissed about this or that, but I don't remember a whole lot. I think I may be different than other players, because I really wasn't concerned with who the manager was—I really was more concerned about just playing."

Despite his intensity, playing for Billy was not without its light moments.

"I remember one time when I was doing [poorly], I got called into Billy's office by [coach] Clete [Boyer]," Mike Pagliarulo recalled. "When Clete came up to you and said, 'Billy wants to see you,' you're either going to get sent down or it would be something off the wall.

"'Billy wants to see you,' he told me, and I said, 'Oh, Jeez.' So I went in there—and I was playing poorly—and Billy said, 'Listen, kid, you dumbass dago. Listen, I want you to go out. I'm getting in at 2:30 and I want you to go out tonight. You're playing tomorrow. If you're in before me, though, it's going to cost you $1,000.'

"He said, 'Now get your boys over there, [Dave] Righetti and Mattingly, and go on out and have a good time and you're playing tomorrow.' Then he said, 'By the way, forget Mattingly—we need him tomorrow.' So Righetti came up to me, we went out, I was pie-eyed, I don't know what happened.

"The next day, I hit a home run and I got two hits. I was sitting on the bench and I said, 'Billy, tell me I don't have to do that again.' He said, 'No, go home and get some rest. What are you, crazy?'"

Piniella was clearly another fiery guy. He was also the guy who, as the batting coach, showed Mattingly a weight shift that could—and did—produce more power.

Piniella, always a guru of hitting, was the Yankees manager in 1986, '87, and '88 before the final reign of Billy Martin.

"I liked playing for Lou, too," Mattingly said. "I played *with* Lou. He was the hitting coach, and then he was the manager. I didn't pay that much attention—just tried to go out and play and not really think about what Lou's like. I just kind of know Lou for being Lou. I really credit him with teaching me how the swing worked. He helped me develop power by teaching me how to really use my bottom hand. He really blessed me since that knowledge helps me teach, because I understand what happens in the swing, what causes what. He taught me that."

When asked who was his best dugout manager, Mattingly was undecided. "You know what? I don't know," he said. "When I played, I didn't pay much attention early on. It's not like I was a bench guy, sitting there analyzing why we're doing this or why we're doing that. As you get a little older you start getting a feel for it. I always looked at the manager and if he had a team going in the right direction. You can't really build chemistry, but you put a team together that plays a certain way—not necessarily in a certain style but one that plays the game the way you want them to play... plays the game right. If you can get everybody on that page and heading in that direction, then you're going to get the most out of them. That's the way I looked at Johnny Oates and guys like him. That's what I took away from him. And when I got older, I started thinking things like, *Why are you bringing in this guy here or that guy there?*"

Mattingly said that the most important thing is the game—and being prepared for it. The constant change in managers and the difficulties of playing in a tough place like New York (something he "loved") weren't the issues. None of it mattered when he was doing the things he needed to do to be a major league player and star.

"People always say, 'The manager this, the manager that,' but the manager never really made a difference in how I played," he said. "He wasn't going to change the way I played, how I got ready to play. Of course, I played for some guys who I liked playing for. I played for Johnny Oates in Triple A [in 1983]. And I thought Buck [Showalter] was a good manager—I learned from all those guys, but there were guys I liked playing for more than others, and you know the reasons why.

"Looking back as a coach now, I was probably a no-maintenance guy. You didn't have to worry about me. I was going to get ready to play. I was going to be ready to play and get myself loose. You didn't have to worry about me not being there or not wanting to play that day. But I wasn't following games along [like a manager would].

"When I got a little older, at the very end of my career, I'd think, *Okay, we need to bring in [Bob] Wickman against this guy.* I was playing first, thinking, *Bring in Wickman, right now, this guy doesn't hit the sinker.* When you're young and you're playing you just want to establish yourself, you want to show people you can play—and you're trying to win games.

"Honestly, I looked at all the peripheral stuff in New York as just peripheral. Being on the field was really what I knew how to do. I was a young kid from Indiana. I felt like I came from a small town that's not that small. But what was so simple to me, in my mind, was I knew how to play—and it didn't matter if it was New York or Columbus or Cleveland.

"It's tough [in New York]. It's demanding there. Then when you go other places you understand why it's tough there. But it's so simple to me—I always thought I knew how to play, and the field was no different there than it was anywhere else. It was the same dimensions.... I still needed a good pitch to hit, I needed to catch ground balls, I needed to do this on a double play. I could take care of that. I knew how to handle that. And everything else, the peripheral, I was probably a little nervous about."

Still, managerial stability—like working under a Showalter or a Joe Torre, can be a positive.

"I had Billy in there three times," Mattingly said. "When I was going through it, I just thought it was normal in New York. But looking back, when Showalter came in things started to become stable. He was there [four] years before Joe came in. Looking back at it now, you can't build an organization if you're going to change your manager every year. You have to have some continuity in there, someone who knows the players. And really, when it comes down to it, you're going to win with players.

"You have to have a guy who leads and steers your club in the right direction. If you can't get your clubhouse together, if the manager can't demand respect in your clubhouse, you're in trouble. But ultimately the players are going to win."

Mattingly said Showalter was what the Yankees needed. "And he knew talent," he said. "I think until that continuity came back, until we had a stable managerial situation, we could hardly grow."

* * *

Many of us have enjoyed the MLB Network for more than just its game coverage and wrap-ups. We love the "Prime 9" features.

One installment picked the major league's team of the 1980s, and the first baseman on that team was unanimous.

"There was a stretch for, what, five or six years—was there really a better hitter in the game [during that time] than Mattingly?" asked former Red Sox lefty Bruce Hurst.

The broadcast explained that Mattingly led all first basemen in the decade in batting average (.323) and slugging percentage.

"He was a hitting machine, and that's the bottom line," said right-hander Dave Stewart.

For the record, Mattingly hit .278 with two homers and 10 RBIs in 58 career plate appearances against Hurst, a tough left-hander, and he batted .327 with no homers and five RBIs in 65 plate appearances against Stewart, a righty. But it was clear what both men thought of No. 23.

Mattingly collected 1,300 hits and won five straight Gold Gloves during the decade.

"Not only was he a great hitter, the guy was unbelievable at first base," said outfielder Jay Buhner, a former teammate. "[He was a] human vacuum cleaner. He didn't miss anything. The guy was always working—he was a workaholic. He knew that there was always something to help him get the extra advantage."

Mattingly, who was interviewed on the program, said simply, "Gotta keep getting better. Gotta keep getting better."

Said former teammate Billy Sample, "Mattingly brought more to the game than just the numbers—and his numbers were really good."

Added Fred Lynn, "He loved the ball up and he just tomahawked that pitch. You could not throw a fastball by him."

Here is the Prime 9 Team of the Eighties:

1B—Don Mattingly
2B—Ryne Sandberg
SS—Cal Ripken Jr.
3B—Mike Schmidt
LF—Rickey Henderson
CF—Dale Murphy
RF—Dwight Evans
C—Gary Carter
P—Jack Morris

Chapter 3

Foundation of a Dynasty

"He hasn't changed. He's the first one here, last one out. A workaholic. You can see it in him as a coach, and we saw it in him as a player. He's done a lot of things for a lot of people. As a hitting coach, he really helped me a great deal. He was there every day, trying to help not only me but everybody else. He had that kind of heart."

—Longtime Yankees catcher Jorge Posada

O f all the crazy things that happened to Don Mattingly during his stay with the Yankees—and there was always something crazy going on in the Bronx—nothing really came close to what happened August 15, 1991.

The haircut.

Stump Merrill, the Yankees manager at the time, reprimanded Mattingly, Steve Farr, Pascual Perez, and Matt Nokes for having their hair too long. Only Mattingly, the team captain, was threatened with being kept off the field if he didn't toe the line. Merrill sent word during batting practice that Mattingly would sit against the Royals if he didn't get his hair cut right then and there, before the game.

"The thing that bothered me about it was the fact that I got singled out," Mattingly said almost two decades later. "Those were the days when everybody had longer hair, the mullet…was going on. We definitely had other guys on the club who had long hair. It was just part of the times.

"Nobody had said anything to me before that moment—not two days beforehand or the day before about getting a haircut. The day of the game, Stumpy tells me, 'If you don't get your hair cut today, you don't play.'

"It stunned me. I didn't know how to respond to it, so I said, 'Let me think about it.' Then I came back and said, 'I'm not playing.' It all came to me and I thought, *It doesn't seem right*. It was right before the game: *Get it cut or you don't play*. Everybody else was in the same boat.

"I really don't know how long it was. I never felt that it was that long but maybe it was. I never really felt like that mattered, anyway.… I came to spring training so many years and always tried to help guys. We'd bring in guys who were out of shape, overweight, guys that had drug problems. George always had a soft heart for those guys—he always liked giving those guys another shot, which is fine. But then I thought, *I come to camp, I'm in shape, not overweight. I play every day, show up on time. I'm basically a no-maintenance guy. I don't ask for anything from anybody. I show up, get ready to play, and play. I do my thing*. That kind of bothered me that they singled me out because of my hair."

"If they'd have said, 'We want you to get your hair cut, get it cut by tomorrow,'" Mattingly said, he would have reacted differently.

But out of the blue, after batting practice, and just before a game was too much for Mattingly.

At the time, George Steinbrenner was under suspension from Major League Baseball. Mattingly doesn't believe Steinbrenner had anything to do with it. The haircut incident brought down embarrassment on management and the franchise. The whole thing was ridiculous—and it was public.

"You know New York. You don't get away with anything," Mattingly said. "Basically, they called me the next day and almost apologized. They called me upstairs and said, 'Hey, we handled that wrong.' I got it cut. I was never a guy who caused trouble.

"But you can't sit here and demand that I get it cut right before a game. That was more of a principle thing. The inference was that I was causing a problem and I was *never* a problem. I thought, *Why me? Why now? And why this way?*"

Mattingly revealed that on the night of the haircut incident, he had earlier asked then-general manager Gene Michael to explore trade possibilities. He was in the first year of a five-year, $19.3 million contract that would take him through the end of his career, and he thought the club might be better off without him.

"Maybe I don't belong in the organization anymore," he told reporters after the game, a 5–1 New York win. "I talked to [Michael] about moving me earlier in the year. He said, 'We'll talk at the end of the year.' Maybe this is their way of saying we don't need you anymore.

"It was kind of silly to me, but we were not winning and it was Stick's club," Mattingly said of Michael. "He wanted an organization that would be puppets for him and do what he wanted."

Merrill said the decision was his, but Mattingly pointed at the general manager, saying, "It's pretty clear where everything comes from. If Stick wanted the players to do exactly what he said, then he should have been the pitching coach, batting coach, and fielding coach. He should have come down there and been a part of it, but taken part of the blame too."

Said Michael at the time, "He's the captain and he's got a big contract. If we asked the captain to get his hair cut, he should get it cut." However, he added, "I don't want to trade Don Mattingly."

He didn't. Mattingly made it through, finishing his career with the Yankees—and then he was able to smile about it later on.

"It ended up being a good thing because they cut it and they auctioned the hair or something," he laughed when adding, "[There were] some great pictures in the *Post* on that. They showed me in the barber's chair. It was hilarious."

Stump Merrill will always be known as the manager who suspended Don Mattingly because the captain wouldn't get his hair cut before a game. But that doesn't mean Merrill didn't admire the guy who played first base for him, even though Mattingly's production had started to go down because of a bad back.

"I don't know anyone in the game who didn't respect him," Merrill said in Mattingly's *Yankeeography* on the YES Network. "We stepped in the cage during batting practice, and you would see every team in the league stop and watch Donnie hit."

* * *

Don Mattingly was asked what it felt like when George Steinbrenner told him prior to the 1991 season that he would be the new Yankees captain. "He wasn't the one who told me," Mattingly told WFAN's Mike Francesa after Steinbrenner passed away. "I think it was [manager] Stump Merrill.

"At the time, to be honest with you, I didn't really know how to take it, in the context of the importance of it. But over time you really come to cherish that. It's one of those things…the New York Yankees felt you had the leadership qualities [but] you never look at yourself like that.

"I felt I just went out, did my job, and tried to be myself all the time. I tried to help different guys at different times and just did what you did as a person and as a player to help another guy. For the organization to [name me captain is] something that I'm really proud of."

* * *

Buck Showalter was asked how much Don Mattingly helped him restore the "Yankees way" when Showalter took over as manager in 1992.

He offered the answer almost before the question was finished: "To the *Mattingly* way, how's that?" the now manager of the Baltimore Orioles said soon after getting his new job. "It was one and the same."

"Donnie was one of those guys who realized the weight his words carried," Showalter said. "And he measured them. It was like E.F. Hutton— if Donnie approached the subject, everybody listened because they knew it was going to be reality.

"Let's face it, leaders define reality, and you have to pick your spots. And it was important for players to please Donnie. You want that type of guy."

Showalter, a minor league teammate of Mattingly's, was also a first baseman. "In the minor leagues, we played together—and believe me, he was a guy who made me realize I wasn't going to be the next first baseman/ left fielder for the Yankees, because once I saw him I said, 'Okay, I better move on to something else. It's not going to happen,'" he said.

Showalter wound up managing in the Yankees system and was a coach with the big-league club in 1990. He then replaced Stump Merrill, and suddenly some stability came to the most unstable job in sports.

And he did it with Mattingly's help. "I don't ever forget for a second how much easier he made my path," Showalter said. "Donnie would handle things behind the scenes. That's why [when] people say, 'Well, this guy's not really vocal, not really boisterous,' [I say,] 'Do you know what goes on in a plane, in the locker room, and during a game?' Donnie was special. There are not many people like him.

"I think Donnie [understood] what had gone on there. It worked out. He made my path a lot easier. He gave me credibility. I had a lot of guys [who I] managed and coached, but having Don support me was important. There's a reason why he played for the Yankees and nobody else. He was a pretty loyal guy—not a blind loyalty, but you'd better bring it."

Showalter doesn't even want to think about what his life would have been like without Mattingly there and in his corner.

"I remember we were going through some things, and a lot of the media didn't want me to hit him third, or whatever, and Donnie came in and said, 'Hey, do what you have to do.' Donnie had no ego. I can sincerely say this—he equated whether or not he had a good day at the ballpark with whether or not the Yankees won.

"I've seen him sincerely happy after a win and he was 0-for-4, and I've seen him sincerely unhappy after he was 4-for-4 and we lost. You look up 'sincere' in the dictionary and they should have a picture of him. There wasn't any false bravado.

"I remember that it was so comfortable to take players from other teams, knowing that Donnie was going to put his arms around them and say, 'I understand where you're coming from and what went on there, but here we do it this way and it helps us win. We'd like you to be on board with this, [because] you can help us win.' No one ever took it personally—there was never an agenda with Donnie, other than an agenda of winning. You can't put that on a stat sheet.

"If he was hitting .260 with 10 home runs, he was hitting third and people thought, 'What's going on?'.... He could *will* things to happen, I really believe that. And when you play games seven days a week for almost eight months, those things show up on the scoreboard and in the standings. He created a culture of 'team first'...I brought [Derek] Jeter and [Jorge] Posada and [Mariano] Rivera. Those guys were with us during the playoffs. A couple of them were there and not even eligible, but I wanted them to be a part of that environment, and a lot of it was being around Donnie every day.

"Derek still talks about, 'I didn't think there was anything else *but* us being in the playoffs, after coming up there and absorbing Donnie and his presence.' I think he *still* affects what's going on there. And the real challenge the Yankees are going to have is when that core of people Donnie affected is gone. I hope it affects the heck out them, quite frankly." (Showalter's Orioles face the task of rising in the same division as the Yankees.)

There were several times during his four years in the Yankees dugout when Showalter counted on and got Mattingly's help.

"I remember [Ruben] Sierra hit a home run when we first acquired him, and he basically almost low-fived me in the dugout—that's how far he had peeled out [coming out of the box]," Showalter said. "And I looked at Donnie and he said, 'I got it.' He just grabbed Ruben and said, 'Hey, Rube, a great home run, but, hey, we don't do that here. Act like you've hit a home run before and by the grace of God you might hit one again. Just run around the bases and get ready for the next inning. We won't [show] anybody up.' And Ruben said, 'You got it, Cap.'

"Those are the kinds of things that I didn't have to get to. There was just a little look I could give Donnie, and he'd basically say, 'I saw it, I got it.' If it ever gets to my plate, then we've probably got an issue. It was important for the players to please Donnie, to play the game the way he knew it had to be played in order for us to win."

While Showalter appreciated Mattingly, the player also knew that the manager was in charge of a team that was going to turn things around.

"Showalter was good at seeing young talent," Mattingly said. "Bernie [Williams] was coming, [Andy] Pettitte was starting to show up. [Showalter] was talking about [Derek] Jeter, he was talking about Mariano [Rivera]. You heard those names coming...and [Jorge] Posada, and you see a couple of those guys in spring. But at the same time, we had [Paul] O'Neill—he was huge—and Jim Abbott and Jack McDowell...Spike Owen...Mike Gallego. You don't think of all those guys. We had Boggsie over there. We started getting guys that were bothered when we lost. We cared that we lost and we started getting some character."

The Yankees were 76–86 in Showalter's first year and improved to 88–74 in 1993. They were 70–43 and leading the AL East by 6½ games when the labor dispute wiped out the rest of the 1994 season. Then, of course, the Yankees rallied late in 1995 and went to the playoffs—Mattingly's only postseason appearance. The captain was red-hot during a 19–4 finish that wrapped up the first American League wild card spot.

"I remember that team coming back after '94, kind of feeling like it had been cheated, and then getting off to a really sluggish start," said Jack Curry, who covered the team for the *New York Times*. "And I remember Showalter saying that they kind of came back and almost played like a team that [felt as if they] deserved something, and that's why they got off to a slow start, as opposed to a team that should have been hungrier. They almost came back like champions, even though they weren't. They weren't the champions of anything [since] there was a strike season."

Mattingly's numbers decreased during Showalter's stay in New York, but it didn't matter to the manager.

While Rivera and others thought Mattingly should have hung around for at least one more year—the Yankees won it all in 1996—Showalter disagreed.

"That's not true," he said. "I'll tell you about a conversation I had with Donnie. There's about two weeks to go in the season. We had one of the best Septembers in Yankees history to get into the playoffs in '95. But Donnie came in and I saw him getting there at 11:00, 12:00, 1:00 [and saw] all the things he had to go through with his back to get to the point where he could play. I used to talk to him and say, 'Donnie, I'd like you to back off a little bit with some of the work, the back,' and he said, 'Buck, I cannot stand in the batter's box and think I have not outworked and out-prepared the guy I'm facing. I get such a mental edge looking out there and knowing there's no way this guy prepared himself like I have for this moment.'

"With that being said, I couldn't take that essence away from him. But Donnie's back was so bad the last year and I knew it but didn't make it public knowledge. He came in with about two weeks to go [in the season] and said, 'Listen, I'm going for it. I just want you to know. I'm going to let it fly with the back.... I may play one game, I may play the rest of the season. I don't know. But I have to do some things here physically to get us where we need to go.' And I'm telling you what—I got to see the old Mattingly for two weeks and it was like, *Wow!*

"I remember the media asking, 'What's going on with Mattingly? What have you all done?' And I so badly wanted to say, 'Well, take a good look at it, because at the end of the year he's probably not going to be able to scratch his ass.' Every day, I thought, *Okay, he made it through another day.*

"Everybody was saying, 'Why couldn't he have made it one more year?' and then he could have been part of that '96 thing," Jim Leyritz said, "but people didn't realize that Donnie got up at 8:00 in the morning, 9:00 in the morning, went down to the pool, had to do a bunch of exercises in the pool—probably anywhere from five to six hours a day before he even went to the park. He had to do all types of conditioning and exercises just to be able to walk around and move because his back was in such bad shape."

* * *

Back in 1995—long before they would become known as the Core Four—Derek Jeter, Mariano Rivera, Andy Pettitte, and Jorge Posada were four young players all making their big league debuts.

Jeter, age 21, got his first 48 at-bats that year. Rivera, 25, was 5–3 in 19 games, including what would be the only 10 starts of his Yankees career. Posada got one at-bat on his September recall. Pettitte, 23, went 12–9 with a 4.17 ERA and was the only one of the four who played the entire season with Mattingly.

Yet Don Mattingly made an impression on all of them.

Later, Mattingly would be a spring training instructor, and in 2004 he became a coach with the club. First the hitting coach and then the bench coach, Mattingly had an inarguable effect on the Core Four throughout the bulk of their careers.

It was in Jeter's first year, 1995, that Mattingly left one of his first marks.

Walking on one of the back fields during spring training, Mattingly observed Jeter walking off the field. He admonished Jeter not to walk off the field "because you never know who's watching". It's a story that has gained quasi-folklore status over the years, but it's true.

"It happened," Jeter said. "We were at spring training in Fort Lauderdale. We were on a back field and we didn't go on the trip, so we had to go from the back field and walk across the main field to get to the clubhouse. That's what he said: 'You better run, because you never know who's watching.'"

It was a small thing, perhaps, but the kind of thing a veteran leader tells a young player. It was the kind of thing Mattingly had told his teammates.

"A lot of us coming up looked up to Donnie," Jeter said. "He's someone we tried to emulate—not necessarily how he played, but how he went about his business.

"Donnie was the lead-by-example guy. He went out, he played hard, he played every day, and he enjoyed competing."

"Mattingly didn't say much—at least when I got here," Rivera said. "He didn't have to say anything, because his presence was just there [in] his attitude, the way he conducted himself, the way he went about his business.

"He was, to me, a tremendous role model. I admired him in a lot of different ways in the game. Seeing him prepare himself for the game, practice, being in the clubhouse, being the captain of the team... [he is] a tremendous, tremendous guy."

For Jeter, who was a Yankees fan growing up, the chance to play with Mattingly would have been enough for him. The fact that Mattingly turned out to be a great guy was a bonus.

Rivera thinks Mattingly should have tried to play another year so that he could have gotten that elusive championship (something, of course, that may not have happened without Tino Martinez, who signed when Mattingly decided to leave). The pitcher remembers an added benefit of his early days with the club.

"[My locker] was next to [his] in the clubhouse," Rivera said. "It was wonderful knowing that you had Don Mattingly next to you. He was just always there for you, even though I was a rookie.

"What impressed me was the way he took care of himself—on the field, off the field, doing his job, day in and day out. I always thank God for the people I have around me. I appreciate what's happened in my life and that God put people like Don Mattingly in it."

Posada agrees that Mattingly was always there for his mates, regardless of the player's stature with the team.

"He was a leader who cared," Posada said. "He came over and talked. He was a guy I admired growing up, and he went out there and never made excuses, even though he was banged up. There were a lot of things that he did on the field without saying a word."

He just made things easier for the young guys. "He did," Pettitte said. "You appreciate that as a young player, that's for sure. It was great to be there in his last year, to see him finally go the playoffs in that last year and see how excited he was. I think that was his 13th year, and he had never been there before.... I was happy to see that."

Pettitte said he could see what Mattingly was going through, trying to stay on the field with a bad back.

"You knew he wasn't feeling great," Pettitte said, noting the pain that wasn't enough to stop the determined Mattingly. "You just go out and do your job. If you can get on the field, you get on the field. That's just how he was. If your numbers suffer sometimes, that's okay because sometimes you'd rather [have] him at 70 percent than have somebody else at 100 percent.

"I think it's just the same old thing—you want to earn your salary, you get paid to do a job. He went out and played every day, and he played every day hard. I think anybody can learn from that."

When Mattingly, at that time the hitting coach in 2004 and 2005, welcomed the rookies to the big time, the dynamic had shifted.

"It was different," Rivera said. "I didn't interact too much with him because he was on the field and I was in the bullpen, but I definitely knew the help he was to the hitters. He's a tremendous human being, and that's the most important thing."

The consensus among the Core Four—and just about anyone else you talk to in baseball—is that Mattingly has never changed. He never acted like the star he was.

"Never. That's one of the things that impressed me the most," Posada said. "When you talk about Don Mattingly, you're talking about one of the premier players in the league—and he's out there, the first one out there working, the first one out there trying to get the team better. He was always one of us.

"He hasn't changed. He's the first one here, last one out. A workaholic. You can see it in him as a coach, and we saw it in him as a player.

"He's done a lot of things for a lot of people. As a hitting coach, he really helped me a great deal. He was there every day, trying to help not only me but everybody else. He had that kind of heart."

* * *

Bob Klapisch, a columnist for the *Record* in New Jersey, remembered Mattingly in a 1997 column:

> NEW YORK – This was mid-summer, 1995, when Darryl Strawberry was still a stranger in the Yankees clubhouse. He remembers entering a room that, aside from David Cone, was thick with silence. It was not exactly a hostile room, but Strawberry realized he was facing a miniature social crisis.
>
> "I was not sure if anyone wanted to be my friend," said the outfielder, who was returning to New York as a two-time drug offender and a convicted tax felon—so alienated from the baseball community even Buck Showalter kept his distance. But that changed the moment Don Mattingly approached and offered his hand.
>
> The Yankees captain realized he was expending enormous political capital, but he was also firm in his belief that everyone, even Strawberry, deserved a second chance. All Mattingly asked from Darryl was that he play hard. The contract, simple and non-verbal, was sealed with their handshake in the middle of the locker room.
>
> "I wanted Darryl to know that I did not care what happened in the past, that as long as he was ready to play ball, he was welcome in our clubhouse," Mattingly said. "I knew exactly what I was doing and what I was saying. I knew that if I was on Darryl's side, it would be easier for him to make it in the Bronx. That is what I wanted."
>
> That peace treaty is the reason why Strawberry said, "I will always respect Donnie. [I will] always remember him in a good way."

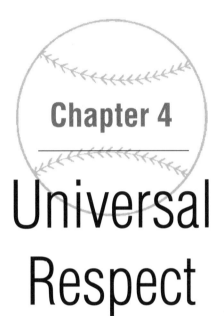

Chapter 4

Universal Respect

"When I was a kid and I idolized him, he had this presence. If you were to draw up a baseball player, I'd say it would be Don Mattingly. Even his mustache was cool. I mean, everything about him [was cool]. He looked great with his glove dangling, the way he wore his uniform. Everything about him represented what you'd call a big-league ballplayer."

—Jason Giambi, former Yankees first baseman

When writing a biography about any subject, the author looks for both sides of the story. Let's face it—not everything about any person can be positive. You talk to people and get the good stuff, but you also hear things that make you frown. After all, no one is liked and respected by everyone.

The funny thing, though, is that Don Mattingly comes as close to beloved as you are going to get.

"I'm sure I have people who don't like me," he said. "I probably have plenty of enemies. But I don't worry about any of that stuff."

If Mattingly has plenty of enemies, this author certainly couldn't find any of them. "And you won't," said Don Baylor.

That's why so many people are rooting for Mattingly to succeed in his new endeavor.

* * *

Players, coaches, the media, and fans weren't the only ones who recognized what kind of player Don Mattingly was during his 14-year career with the New York Yankees.

The umpires noticed, too.

"Donnie was such a good player, and he had such respect throughout the game. I think that's what you admire him for more than anything else— his work ethic," said former umpire Steve Palermo.

"You watched him and you saw him play hard and he would be 4-for-4 in a game but he still wanted to get to 5-for-5. If he didn't put five good at-bats together, it [felt] like a wasted day for him, [even if] he went 4-for-5. That's what you admired about him more than anything else, his professional approach, how he took the game, and the respect that he had for the game."

"Mattingly was always very professional," said Palermo's fellow umpire Rich Garcia. "He was very focused on what he was supposed to do as opposed to what everybody else was supposed to do. He was certainly a good team player, very respectful and very professional dealing with the umpires and dealing with me. He was always very respectful with me."

Palermo said Mattingly's approach helped the umpires work their games.

"He would grab the young kids when he got to be a veteran guy," he said. "He used to pull them off to the side and say, 'Hey, you can't blame the umpire. He's going to get one, you're going to get one, and it's what you decide to do with the other,'" Palermo said as he sat in Fenway Park, working as an umpiring supervisor. "That was his approach. He wasn't an alibi-er, he didn't complain—he just went about his job. I think that's what you admired about him more than anything else."

"He was such a hard worker," said former American League umpire Jim McKean. "I really believe he was an overachiever. He hit a lot of home runs, and I don't really believe he was a home run hitter. He was always very serious, very conscientious, and he worked very hard at what he did, so it's very hard to get a whole lot of negativity out of people who take the job so seriously.

"He didn't necessarily get along with everybody on the field. I was not his best friend, but I think he respected me for what I did, and I respected him for what he did. As far as being friendly, day in, day out, he got a lot more friendly after he retired."

Offered Garcia, "The only time I ever remember him saying anything about any pitches was during one game in Minnesota where [Bert] Blyleven was pitching. I believe he had something like 12 or 14 strikeouts that night. I think I called [Mattingly] out on strikes, and he started complaining about it. My answer to him was, 'Donnie, you're not the first guy he's struck out. This guy throws strikes to everybody.'

"As far as I can remember that was the only time. Normally he was the guy who would come in and calm things down if there was some sort of altercation going on with one of his players or the manager. He would see the umpire get a little hot, and he would be the first one to come in and talk to him in a mild manner and try to get him [to calm] down."

Mattingly remembered having a good relationship with the umps.

"You argue sometimes, [but]I just looked at it like, whatever happened, I was just reacting out there. I think I tried to be respectful of what they had to do. As you get a little older, you're not so wild out there—wild in thinking about winning the game."

Palermo noticed. He said recently, "[Mattingly] learned from good people, too. He had a lot of guys around him who taught him to play the right way. When Billy [Martin] was there, [Mattingly] saw the good, the bad, the ugly—all of it. I think that's what made him a professional player. He understood what it meant to be a Yankee.

"That's not to say that people who play for other organizations don't have great respect for the game. But [Mattingly] understood the history of the game and I think that's what you appreciate more than anything else. There's a reason why he is still in the game, why he's a very respected coach in the game now, and why he's working for a very respected manager. There's a reason why [Joe Torre] wants you on his staff.

"I'm sure it took a lot for Mattingly to leave the Yankees organization and New York to go out to L.A. with Joe. He likes working under a guy like Joe Torre."

"You have to be able to talk to [umpires]," Mattingly said, something that will be further tested as he starts his managerial career. "They're part of the process—and I think, looking at it now, these guys are part of the game. You need to be respectful of them."

Neither McKean, Palermo, nor Garcia can remember ever tossing Mattingly from a game.

"It never got to that point," McKean said. "He wasn't a pain in the ass, and he wasn't a constant griper. He just worked very hard, and he expected everybody out there to work with him, which is a little different than you see today.

"He would [have his gripes], but he's one of those guys at the beginning of the game he'd say, 'Hi, Jim.' It was business from then on. He took the game very seriously, which probably is going to make him a good manager.

"He has a lot of the traits that good managers have today—they work very hard, are very conscientious, and respect the game. He's got a lot of Buck Showalter in him, he's got a lot of Tony La Russa in him—the type of manager who's very serious and takes the job seriously but with great production. He was never a player to hit 400- or 450-foot home runs. He was always a guy who hit them 320, 330, which tells me that he has very good mechanics and did his job very well."

Said Garcia, "I can't remember running him [out of a game]. If I did, I think I would remember. He was always very respectful, and he was a good player. Most of the time, you don't have problems with good players because they're very focused on what they're supposed to be doing. It's not that they don't argue, it's not that they don't have any sort of drive, it's just that they're very focused on what they're supposed to be doing and they're good at it.

"I remember once I was screaming at Matt Nokes going to the locker room after a game. [Mattingly] came over and put his arm around me and said, 'The game's over. Calm down.' That's the kind of guy he was. He was a peacemaker, more or less."

It's clear that Mattingly respected the guys who made the calls.

"I think I learned early on how to talk to them—especially at home plate about the strike zone," Mattingly said. "I feel like I had to talk to them—I had to let them know that I was seeing the baseball. That was my biggest thing. If I felt a ball was a little bit off, I wanted to question it—not by saying, 'That ball's out,' but more that it's always different. Each strike to me is different. On a first strike, if that ball's just a little bit off and he gives it to [the pitcher], I'm okay with that, but I'll keep my head down and say, 'Is that ball right? Did that ball nick the corner out there? Did that ball just hit the corner right on the edge out there?' Or, 'Is that as high as we're going there?' if I thought a ball was up.… I wanted to learn to do that. I wanted to let the umpire know that I knew the strike zone, that I was seeing the ball. I always felt that when I was seeing the ball, I knew if a pitch was 2 inches off. If I'm seeing the ball well, and pitcher throws one that's *that* far off, I know it's a ball.

"Now, when I was pulling off or cheating or going through stretches where I came out quickly, I would think the ball's away and then look out there and realize, *Man, I'm pulling off somewhere here.* But when I was in there and staying on the ball and I wasn't moving, I knew if that pitch was a ball or a strike. Sometimes, it was down or up [from what I thought], but I knew *off* for sure. It was the same thing with in—every once and a while on a ball in, I got fooled a little bit.

"So I wanted to make sure [the umpires] knew that the balls were out. First strike's one way, second strike's another way of talking, for me—the second strike puts you in danger. I might say, 'Hey, that ball's off. That ball's 2 inches off.' I wanted the umpire to know that I'm seeing the ball clearly, because the ball was barely off—I knew it was close, but it wasn't a strike. My biggest thing was close is not a strike. If it's close to the edge, it doesn't mean it's a strike. It has to be on the plate."

Mattingly smiles when he talks about getting ejected. "Every once and a while I'd get a little crazy during a game," he recalled. "I got tossed probably five or six times in my entire career. A lot of times I'd get tossed late in the game when I just didn't want to be in there anymore. Times when we were getting killed and I felt like, *Okay, I've had enough.* You know if you want to go or not. I knew if I kept going I was going to get thrown in probably half of the times I got tossed.

"Tim Welke got me at home plate once in Texas. [Joe] Brinkman got me. I remember that one clearly. He got me at the start of a doubleheader against Kansas City. I was struggling but I was starting to swing the bat really well, and I had done well against the two pitchers that were throwing for Kansas City. I thought, *You know what? I have to get ready for the whole day*, because I was getting eight, ten at-bats, instead of four.

"You know that first at-bat when there's only 400 people in the stands at a doubleheader because nobody's there yet? Brinkman called me out, first freakin' time up, on a ball that had to be 6 inches off the plate. It just drove me [nuts]. I walked away saying, 'That's not a freakin' strike.' If he had just let it go, I would have let it go, too. I'd have been mad still, but he said, 'Ball's there!' It just made me mad. The guy told me it was a strike when I knew it wasn't a strike. That really irritated me. When it's not close—if it's a nick here or there, I'd think, *Maybe I'll give him the benefit of the doubt*, but some of them I knew were balls and not strikes. Those were usually the ones I got [ejected] on.

"I played in the second game, and I hit a double on my first at-bat. I was sliding into second, and he was the umpire standing over me. As soon as I slid into second, he was standing over me. But you have to let it go. And usually, with most umpires, what I tried to do if I got thrown out was come up the next day and say, 'Hey, my bad. I just lost it.' You can't take anything like that personally. It can't be a vendetta-type thing. It just doesn't work like that. You'd see those guys over and over. For the most part, they're trying to do their best. It doesn't matter what they do, somebody's going to be pissed—either one side or the other."

Mattingly does not name names as far as the umpires he didn't care for, but he does recall a few of the stronger umpires who stood out.

"When I was playing, I thought Welke was really good," he said. "[Ken] Kaiser was good when he wanted to be. When the game was on the line, Kaiser was good. If it was out of hand, he'd say, 'Let's go, it's a strike.'

"If you come up as a young guy, bitching and arguing stuff, you're going to get killed. I knew as a young guy to shut my mouth and take it. Once you establish yourself, you get a little credibility. People think, *Okay, he can play here. This guy can hit and he knows the strike zone.* But if you're a young guy they would call some [marginal] stuff, especially if it was a veteran pitcher and a young kid. It's not like today. Back then that went on for sure."

Speaking about the negative side of umpiring, Mattingly said, "I'm not going to badmouth any umpires."

"I will say, in general and still even today, the guys who you don't like are the guys who umpire as if they don't care. Like, *I don't care. I don't want to talk about it, I'm right all the time.*'

"If the guy's giving you effort out there, he's trying his hardest, he can get mad but he can't really get mad. You know what I mean? As opposed to a guy who is really good, but he's just kind of arrogant [who projects an attitude like] *Whatever. That ball's down. No, in.* You can't even talk to him. That's the kind of umpire who irritates you [as a batter] because it seems like they just don't care.

"I want the guy who's trying to do his best and giving me his best effort. It's like a player. A guy's going out, busting his butt, and he's giving you everything he's got. If he's giving you everything he knows how to give and trying as best as he can, it's hard to really get on the guy. You know he's giving you everything he's got—and when you get that from an umpire, it's no problem."

McKean said he did have one problem with Mattingly—one negative on a long list of positives. "One thing Don did, in my mind, was hit home runs when I didn't want them as an umpire," he said. "He was a big-time clutch hitter—at least it seemed like that when I umpired. There were a couple of guys in baseball who were like that—Rod Carew was like that, Wade Boggs was like that. They were very good hitters in the seventh, eighth, and ninth innings. I don't have numbers to look at to prove I'm correct, but it always seemed like that to me. When you didn't need a hit [as an umpire], [Mattingly] was the kind of guy you could count on to make good contact and get a hit somewhere.

"I appreciated [what he did] as a ballplayer. I didn't appreciate it as an umpire because he used to ruin a lot of games for me. A lot of 3–2s turned into 3–3s, and we were [out] there for a while. But I could count on those types of guys. There were certain guys you just didn't want to see late in the game. We all have those."

In other words, Mattingly and others like him messed up some dinner plans or plane reservations?

"He was a *bad* guy to have up there, which means he was a very good clutch hitter," McKean said with a laugh.

McKean has noticed a change in Mattingly since his playing days. "I heard or thought I saw more things come out of the dugout from him [as a coach] than I did as a player. [As a player,] you wouldn't hear much from him in the dugout. He was more on the field, more right down to the job. But I've noticed more chirping from the dugout [now that he is a coach]. I never noticed much of that as a player. I noticed far more of that when he was a coach."

Perhaps he was just getting ready for managing. "Yeah, it's called preparation," McKean said.

"That I don't know. I really can't say. I don't have any evidence of that," Garcia said. "I haven't really seen it.

"When you're sitting in the dugout watching and you're responsible for certain things, you have more time to analyze things as opposed to analyzing your [own] stance, the strike zone, what the pitcher's throwing. That's why I say that when he was playing he was focused on what *he* was doing as opposed to focusing on what the umpire or the coaches or the manager were doing. He was focused on that pitcher that particular day and the game itself. If that's the case today, I attribute that to the fact that he's got too much time on his hands," he concluded, laughing.

As far as predicting success in Mattingly's managerial future, both McKean and Garcia agree that Mattingly brings the necessary tools and approach to the job.

While best known for his uniform No. 23, which was retired by the Yankees in 1997, Mattingly wore No. 46 during the 1982 and 1983 seasons. Here he waits on deck during the July 4, 1983, game against the Red Sox at Yankee Stadium. Dave Righetti pitched a no-hitter for the Yankees that day. (Diamond Images/ Getty Images)

Mattingly accepts congratulations from Yankees manager Yogi Berra after hitting his first career home run at Yankee Stadium on April 24, 1984. (AP Images)

Mattingly knocks out another hit in September 1984. The Yankees first baseman won the American League batting title that year, edging out teammate Dave Winfield in Mattingly's first full major league season. (AP Images)

Don Mattingly certainly had fun in 1985, leading the American League with 48 doubles and 145 RBIs. (Ronald C. Modra/Sports Imagery/Getty Images)

Three of baseball's greatest left-handed hitters—(from left) Wade Boggs, Ted Williams, and Don Mattingly—discuss the art of hitting in March 1986. (Ronald C. Modra/Sports Imagery/ Getty Images)

With son Taylor in his arms, Mattingly meets reporters at Yankee Stadium after being named the 1985 American League Most Valuable Player. (AP Images)

Mattingly (right) jokes around with teammates Dave Winfield (left) and Rickey Henderson during spring training in 1987. Winfield and Henderson were later voted into the Baseball Hall of Fame. (Keith Torrie/NY Daily News Archive via Getty Images)

Yankees owner George Steinbrenner (center) shares the dugout with manager Billy Martin (left) and general manager Lou Piniella during spring training in 1988. Mattingly recalls all three men as major influences in his life. (AP Images)

Three of the majors' best first basemen—(from left) Keith Hernandez of the Mets, Mark McGwire of the Athletics, and Mattingly—talk shop before the 1987 All-Star Game. Mattingly and Hernandez starred at the same position in New York during the 1980s, setting off debates about who was the better player. (Focus On Sport/Getty Images)

Always a rock 'n roll fan, Mattingly sported longer hair in 1991. In August of that season, Yankees manager Stump Merrill benched his team captain for refusing to cut his hair.
(Mitchell Layton/Getty Images)

Mattingly (right) chats with Yankees manager Buck Showalter (left) and owner George Steinbrenner in spring training in 1993. After a seemingly never-ending revolving door of managers throughout Mattingly's career, Showalter's four-year run provided stability and a playoff appearance in 1995.
(AP Images)

Mattingly won nine Gold Gloves for his excellence at first base. Here he dives to tag Texas' Otis Nixon during a July 1995 game. (AP Images)

The Yankees celebrate after clinching the American League wild card on October 1, 1995. Mattingly hit safely in the final 10 games of the regular season. (Greig Reekie/ AFP/Getty Images)

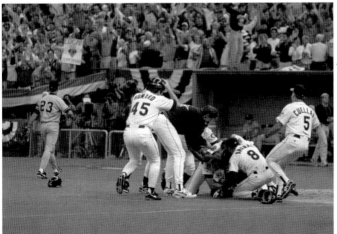

Don Mattingly (far left) walks off the field for the final time as a player following the Mariners' crushing extra-inning Game 5 win that advanced them to the 1995 American League Championship Series. (Stephen Dunn/Getty Images)

Mattingly leaves the batter's box after his home run in Game 2 of the 1995 American League Division Series. He batted .417 in his only career postseason series. (AP Images)

"He's going to have great determination, and I know he's going to work as hard as he can work, I will say that," McKean said. "The only thing that he's going to have to adjust to is that not everybody plays the game like he played it. That's been very frustrating for a lot of young managers—guys who go from player to manager, [looking] for guys who played the game like they did, which is to play the right way. A lot of guys don't [play that way], and that's a frustration for managers that sometimes creates a lot of problems."

"I always thought that [Mattingly] would be [a manager]," Garcia said. "I've always thought that he has that kind of ability. He has a lot of leadership qualities—and not necessarily in the *rah-rah* way but just the way he played the game. He played hard every day and gave it all he had.

"Frankly I thought that he would someday end up being the Yankees manager. I'm kind of surprised that this is the route [he's] going."

Many think Mattingly would have managed the Yankees had George Steinbrenner remained at the helm of the team's operations.

"[Steinbrenner] was a big fan of Mattingly and I think George always had that in the back of his mind—that Donnie would be the manager of the Yankees someday," Garcia said. "[Mattingly is] a throwback. We need more guys in the game like him. I was very happy to hear that he's going to manage the Dodgers."

* * *

Mark Gubicza was 132–136 during a 14-year major league career (all but one decision for the Kansas City Royals) that included a 20–8 season and two trips to the All-Star Game. Hall of Famer Rod Carew went 1-for-10 against him; Reggie Jackson was 2-for-15; Rickey Henderson batted .229; Kirby Puckett .238.

On average, the Hall of Famers batted .274 against him. They hit eight home runs in 596 at-bats, none hitting more than two.

Don Mattingly was 33-for-80 (.413) against the right-hander, with four homers, 17 RBIs, a .663 slugging percentage, and a 1.106 OPS.

"For me, he was the toughest hitter. He and Wade Boggs [.367 against Gubicza] were the two guys I had the most difficult time with," said Gubicza, now a broadcaster with the Angels, the same team with which he finished his career. "But Mattingly [was the toughest] in particular, because he could drive the ball out of the ballpark. [That] made it more difficult.

"I knew if I came inside, that if I didn't get way in, it was going to be pulled and be out of the ballpark. Then he had really good power to left-center field—even in our [big] ballpark in Kansas City. I remember as his back started going out everyone said, 'Just throw the ball away, he'll hit a lazy fly ball to left.' Well, every time I tried doing that he still ended up getting a hit off of me.

"He was probably my most difficult out, as far as the number of at-bats and the success he had against me.

"I had success against some other guys on the team, guys who were really good hitters on the Yankees. But for whatever reason he saw the ball well out of my hand. There was no rhyme or reason about it. There were even a couple of times when I turned around and laughed at him after he got his third or fourth hit off me in a game. He'd look at me and say, 'I don't know how I did it, either.' But some guys just get comfortable or see the ball well. Some guys have success or luck, and he just happened to be one of those guys who had all of the above against me."

As a Royal, Gubicza was taught to hate the Yankees, the team that ousted Kansas City from the playoffs in 1977 and '78 before the Royals finally got their revenge in 1980, all prior to Gubicza's arrival. "When I first came up with Kansas City, George Brett said, '[Even] if we lose every game during the year, as long as we beat the Yankees [in] every game, that's a good year,'" Gubicza said. "So we hated the Yankees [in] Kansas City, and that was a pretty good rivalry for a while. But I couldn't get [Mattingly] out, and I ended up liking him, which made it worse."

It's been a decade and a half since Gubicza faced Mattingly, but one can tell the at-bats are still in the pitcher's mind.

When asked if he remembered Mattingly's home runs, he said, "Oh yeah, I remember them all—especially [the ones] in Yankee Stadium. I think he got me twice in Yankee Stadium, right down the right-field line. And I'm still convinced it's not 308 or 309 [feet]…I always joke and say it was 290.

"I was a sinkerball guy, and I had a really difficult time throwing four-seam fastballs or cut fastballs on the inner half above the belt. I think that's where you could get him. But he used to get his hands through, and he'd be able to tuck his hands in. As soon as I'd see the bat going through as the pitch was delivered, I'd think, *Oh God, that's not going to be a good result at all*, and, *boom*, it went out of the ballpark.

"But I respect him because he's a guy who would hit a home run and run fast around the bases. He didn't show you up. And if I ever got him out, I never showed him up either.

"I love the way he played. I love the way he played defense too. [At that time in baseball, there were many] big, burly guys playing first base, but he wasn't a big guy—and he was the guy who played tremendous defense for them."

Gubicza smiled when he talked about a personal relationship with Mattingly that was formed as teammates on the '88 and '89 All-Star teams and on an All-Star tour of Japan after the 1988 season.

Gubicza knows Mattingly's back woes are the reason he's not in the Hall of Fame, but he still thinks Mattingly belongs there. Gubicza recently told Mattingly at Dodger Stadium, "You better thank me when you get in there because I helped get you into the Hall of Fame with all the base hits and home runs and RBIs you had off me.'

During the Freeway Series—the exhibitions between the Dodgers and Angels—Gubicza said, "Larry Bowa will come up and say, 'Hey, Gooby, there's your buddy,' and start laughing. [Mattingly is] really mellow about it. There's no question he knows the success he had against me. He didn't rub it in, but I always remembered it everywhere I went."

The four homers off Gubicza matched the most Mattingly hit against any pitcher. (He also hit four against Jack Morris, Tom Candiotti, and

Charlie Hough.) But the .413 average was not a Mattingly best. He hit .500 against Scott McGregor, .458 against Pat Hentgen, .447 against Dan Petry, .412 off Jack McDowell, .410 off John Cerutti, and .409 off Bert Blyleven.

Mattingly hit three homers apiece off McGregor, Petry, Moore, and Blyleven—and also poked three each off Mark Langston, Teddy Higuera, Floyd Bannister, Mike Witt, Walt Terrell, Doyle Alexander, and Bob Welch.

He hit .348 against Randy Johnson in the regular season, fanning six times, but the Big Unit struck him out four times in the playoffs, including Mattingly's last at-bat in the major leagues. He batted .311 against Roger Clemens, with six strikeouts in 75 plate appearances. Mattingly never hit a home run against either of the pitchers, but he drove in eight runs against each.

"You could never get a pattern with Donnie," Clemens said. "He'd shoot you to left and pull you to right. As a pitcher, that's difficult to deal with."

Mattingly remembers righty Scott Erickson and lefthander Frank Viola as the pitchers he did *not* want to see. Mattingly was 5-for-29 (.172) against Erickson and 13-for-52 (.180) off Viola.

"I usually throw my whole repertoire at him," Viola told the *New York Times* in 1988. "You've got to mix it up and hope he's not looking for that certain pitch."

During his career, Mattingly faced 10 current Hall of Famers. He batted .309 in 110 at-bats against Nolan Ryan, Tom Seaver, Dennis Eckersley, Don Sutton, Phil Niekro, Rollie Fingers, Steve Carlton, Jim Palmer, Rich Gossage, and Gaylord Perry, but he hit only one home run—off Sutton. He was 7-for-21 against Sutton, and 6-for-14 against Tom Seaver.

He was 6-for-22 against Dennis Eckersley, something Eck is clearly proud of to this day.

"Remembering Mattingly, more than anything, I was just hoping that he'd hit it at somebody when he came up." Eckersley said with a laugh. "[He was that type of hitter], which to me says it all. I thought I could get most everybody out—you have to believe that as a pitcher, confidence-wise— but it's telling when you hope [your batter] hits it at somebody.

"I really didn't have anything to get him out, so he had to get himself out. He didn't swing and miss a lot—at least, I didn't see myself striking him out."

Former closer Jeff Reardon basically said the same thing, noting, "With most hitters, you thought of ways to strike them out—but not with Mattingly. You were just trying to get an out, like [I did] with Pete Rose.

"He was a very tough out. He was one of those guys [from whom] pitchers will take an out any way they can," Reardon said. "For the majority of hitters, a pitcher wants a strikeout, but Mattingly was not one of them."

Added Eckersley, "I don't think you were worried about him taking you bridge [a home run]," he said. "He wasn't one of those guys where it felt like, *Uh-oh, I hope I keep this ball in the ballpark.* Even though he hit his share of home runs, I didn't consider him a home run hitter."

But Eckersley did consider Mattingly a pain. "He was a gap hitter who didn't strike out. He pretty much did whatever the hell he wanted," he said.

Mattingly fanned only twice in 24 plate appearances against Eckersley.

"When I faced him, the Yankees sucked—in '87, '88, '89, '90, they were brutal," Eckersley said, recalling facing Yankees of that era as the dominating closer of the American League's best team. "In 1990 we were like 12–0 against them, which was crazy. We had our way with them. [Oakland outscored New York by a 62–12 margin.] He was their toughest out. It's a lot easier to pitch to somebody when you haven't got a lot of damage in the lineup."

Eckersley recalled a long Mattingly at-bat, which turned out to be the last time the two squared off.

"I think the last time I faced him was in '95," Eck said, recalling his last season in Oakland. "I had a horrific September in '95. I pitched three innings in that game—and I never pitched three innings. I blew the save, so I had to keep going. I had to throw 20 pitches to this guy. [Records show it was actually 10.] I pitched three innings, and after that I sucked the rest of the year. I couldn't get anybody out. I was almost done. I never went three innings before or after."

Catchers felt the same pressure as pitchers when it came to Mattingly. They were the ones who had to call the pitches aimed to get him out.

"There was no pattern with him," said Tony Peña, who played for the Red Sox and Indians against Mattingly and later coached with him in the Bronx. "I remember when I used to call the game, we had to move the ball around. We could not stay in one place. He was the type of guy who made the adjustments. He was a great hitter. Sometimes, it was very, very tough for a catcher or pitcher to figure out.

"He used to spray the ball around. He knew when to use the power, and he became a better power hitter at the end because he started to figure out the ballpark and pulled the ball more. Then when he went away [from home], he would change. I remember we could not pitch Don Mattingly at Yankee Stadium the same way we pitched him anywhere else."

"At the beginning, he had a little bit of a weakness inside," said former Red Sox catcher Gary Allenson, who wound up working in the Yankees organization with Mattingly. "He was more of an opposite-field gap hitter, so we tried to get in on him—although you couldn't stay in there, because obviously he was such a good hitter.

"After I was done playing in '87, I came back and managed in the Yankees system. I came to spring training and he was obviously there, and I asked him, 'How do you approach hitting?' I got probably the most interesting comment I've ever heard. Most everybody times the fastball and makes adjustments to something else. He said that except for [hitting against] a few of the tough lefties, he would stride for the breaking ball.

"Say someone throws 93 mph and their slider is 85. He would stride for something 85 mph—not look for a slider, but stride for the 85 mph pitch and make the adjustment with his hands when he saw the ball. That [strategy] lets the ball get in the hitting zone, a lot more than what I got, obviously. It was a very interesting comment: *Stride for something a little bit slower and then make your hands work.* Too often, especially in my case, I was out in front trying to hit one over there, and if it wasn't a fastball middle-in and thigh high, I was in trouble."

Whatever Mattingly did, it worked—and he worked at the craft harder than anyone.

"In an organization that has had all those home runs hitters, he didn't get locked up in the home run stuff. I think he was, for the most part, a hitter who was concerned with winning a game and not about the home run," Allenson said.

And what made him so special?

"I would say his concentration level," said lefty Mike Flanagan, who held Mattingly to a .265 batting average and yielded no homers. "I felt I had an advantage over most left-handed hitters, but I really didn't against him.

"I had a pretty good sidearm curveball, which was effective on most left-handed hitters. He hit some that were a half a foot, a foot outside that other people wouldn't even come near, and he would drive it the other way. But he was special.

"We really had some great battles over the years. He was such a tough competitor. We had a pretty good rivalry. He hit a grand slam off me in spring training one year—these things didn't go on just during the seasons, they went on even in the preseason. If I remember correctly, I may have hit him with a pitch or something later. So we really did have a sort of grudge match between us, and there was a big rivalry at that time between the Orioles and Yankees.

"He was a remarkable player for a span of six or seven years. There was nobody better. Nobody could hit at a high fastball better. I can remember some of the pitches he hit. He was such a leader and really underestimated as a defensive player."

* * *

Bernie Williams said, "He never gave up. Donnie represents the way baseball should be played."

That representation, and the kind of guy Mattingly was as a player and has been as a coach, allowed him to affect the lives of many young players. Buck Showalter counted on that leadership during the years he managed

Some other Mattingly numbers:

- He hit .314 against right-handers, .296 against left-handers.
- He hit .313 at home, .302 on the road.
- He hit 131 homers at home, 91 on the road.
- He batted .304 in the first half of the season, .311 in the second half.
- He batted .347 in Yankees wins, .263 in losses.
- He hit .292 with the bases loaded, with six grand slams and 127 RBIs.
- He batted .314 with runners in scoring position, .320 with men on base, .387 with a runner on third and less than two outs, .282 with two outs and runners in scoring position, .363 when hitting the first pitch, and .318 in innings seven through nine—.347 in the seventh, .312 in the eighth and .289 in the ninth.
- He hit .304 late in close games, .302 when the score was tied.
- He was just 1-for-5 in his career when putting a 3–0 pitch in play.

the Yankees. Joe Torre has counted on it when Mattingly, named to replace Torre as manager of the Dodgers, worked with him in New York and Los Angeles.

"He never, ever gave away an at-bat," Williams once said. "What I will remember about Donnie is that he taught me to treat every at-bat like it was my first…or last. It is the hardest thing to have total concentration on every day of the season. He was always ready."

That alone made him one of the great Yankees. But there was more—so much more.

When Mattingly joined the Yankees, he was the young guy, the one learning the ropes from people like Rich Gossage, Graig Nettles, Dave Winfield, and company.

"There were lots of guys I looked up to when I played—guys I came up with like Goose Gossage, Lou Piniella, Bobby Murcer," Mattingly said.

"Those guys were tough, and they played the game because they loved it. They played it hard. They got ready to play. They respected it. I learned so much from that whole team."

But it wasn't long after his arrival that Mattingly became the leader of that team and eventually its captain.

"When Bernie Williams came up, Bernie was the target of a lot of awful ribbing and kidding by some not very nice members of the team," recalled broadcaster Suzyn Waldman. "Referring to him as Bambi was the least of it. I knew Bernie very well, so I saw that all and I knew how it upset him and how tentative he was about everything.

"It was Mattingly who sat him down one day and said, 'You belong here, but you have to prove it.' It was Mattingly who told him he was as good as anybody else and not to let everything get him down. And Bernie will credit Don Mattingly with making him the kind of player that he turned out to be.

"Mattingly didn't tell anybody. I knew it because I'm always in the wrong place at the wrong time—or at the right time, depending on what you think—but that's something that people [might not] know. That's the kind of leader that Don Mattingly was and the kind of respect that he got."

It was respect to the point of worship. It was respect to the point that the players on the 1995 team felt worse about Mattingly losing than they did about the actual outcome.

"When Pat Kelly came up to the Yankees [in 1991], I watched him watching Don Mattingly get dressed so that he would put on the uniform exactly right," Waldman said. "He used to sit and watch him, very quietly, just so that he would do [the same thing].

"There were a million of those things. It happened all the time.

"When Wade Boggs came over to the Yankees, everyone said, 'They don't like each other. This is going to be a mess.' On the first or second day of spring training in Fort Lauderdale, I remember being up in the press box and looking out on the field—and there was Mattingly running laps with

Boggs, in front of everybody. I remember thinking to myself, *This is going to work.*

"But *he* did it. Donnie went out of his way. I'm sure Boggs didn't say, 'Let's go running in the outfield.' Mattingly knew what to do, and when Boggs came the team was dead last in on-base percentage. And by the time the season was done, the Yankees were the No. 1 team in walks.… Mattingly went out of his way to say that it was Boggs, that he was the reason."

During his four years in New York, Showalter counted on Mattingly to take care of things before they ever reached the manager. That quality defined Mattingly's leadership.

"Ask O'Neill about him," Showalter said.

Several other former teammates and guys who played when Mattingly was coaching with the Yankees talked about the man they just called "Cap." Here are their memories and insights:

Paul O'Neill

"He was probably the best friend I had when I got there. If you had asked me a week after I got there, he was probably the one guy I gravitated to and talked a lot to. I loved to see his insights on hitting. We became very, very good friends.

"I used to enjoy watching him during a game from my view in right field—just the little things he did, defensively and also moving on pitches. He was a complete baseball player. He wasn't a guy who learned the game late. He was just a smart baseball player. He was so much into the game.

"He was a guy who everybody on our team loved. You never heard a bad thing said about him from the other team, either. A lot of people had a lot of respect for Donnie for the way he went about things and what he was able to accomplish until the injuries came.

"He had the respect of the everyday players. He also was extremely smart and was always into the game. Whether it was Opening Day or whether it was September, he was always into the game. That made

you feel the importance of going out and winning. He was able to have a lot of fun after the game and away from ballpark, too, and those were some of the times I'll remember.

"We talked a lot about hitting, and he really made me believe that I could be successful hitting to all parts of the field again, like I had been comfortable doing at one time. I had become a pull hitter in Cincinnati, trying to hit more home runs. When I heard from him, 'For you to be successful, you have to hit the ball all over,' it made sense to me and it helped me. I had all the respect in the world for him because I saw him work. I knew what he'd been through with some injuries, and I knew what he had been through when he was healthy.

"There are some people in life who are just likeable people, and he was that type of person [and] player.

"I remember going to a movie with him one night in Oakland [in 1995]. I hadn't been hitting very well, and I'd had a horrible game. I said jokingly, 'Cap, am I ever going to get another hit?' He looked at me in the taxi and said, 'Hey, with that tired old swing, probably not.' I just looked over at him. I wanted a little more than that, wanted a little 'You'll be all right.' But that was his way. We laughed about that. I still consider him one of the most fun people and best friends that I've ever played with."

Dave Righetti

"He was considered too short, not big enough or strong enough to do great things. It was just the way he played. He played bigger than he was, and that was his whole career."

Jim Leyritz

"Any chance I get to talk about Cap, I'm ready. He was one of my guys. When the Yankees first signed me, he was one of the first few guys I met. Of course, at that time, he was in his heyday. It was a thrill to be able to meet him.

"I got called up in Baltimore, and when we came home from the road trip, I walked into the stadium for the first time to find out where my locker was and it happened to be right next to his. That was quite a thrill because at the time he was the Yankee, and the captain. I got to sit next to him and take in everything—how he prepared for games, how he got ready, his approach, and everything else.

"He reminded me a lot of Pete Rose. Pete wasn't a great athlete or the best hitter, but he made himself into that. After a game, even if [Mattingly] was 3-for-4, if he didn't feel right, he would go and start hitting. He would spend an hour and a half, two hours after a game. He was just a worker. He made himself into such a great hitter, and it was shame he never got the opportunity to get into the postseason after that first round."

"When you talk about all-around—friendship, being able to take a young kid and say, 'Listen, pick my brain, talk to me'—his accessibility was second to none. [I remember] what he made me feel like as a young player, the things that he taught me. You have to remember, I was coming up as a young player and was playing his position. But even when Donnie was hurt, even when Donnie was on the disabled list, he'd come out to first base and he would teach me. He would say, 'You need to do this. You need to do that. Hold a guy on this way.' Even though he was unable to play, he was out there helping the team one way or the other. I [never] played with anyone else who was like that—especially someone as good as he was who had the reputation he had for being a superstar.

"I played with Tony Gwynn. He wasn't like that. Thinking back on it, I was one of the luckiest players ever, because during that time, Donnie, Wade Boggs, and Tony Gwynn were probably the three greatest hitters of that time, and I got to play with all three of them. When I played with the Yankees, my hitting group was Wade Boggs, Don Mattingly, and me a lot of the time. When you talk about learning, working on things in batting practice, and how to hit, I learned so much *from him and Wade by just being in that group and watching how they approached it. I was kind of disappointed when I went to San Diego. I was expecting Tony to be like Wade and Donnie, and he was completely the opposite."*

"My first ejection from a major league game was because of Don Mattingly. He was on the disabled list, and he was sitting on the bench. We were playing the Angels, and I had hit a home run off Mark Langston, just inside the foul pole. I circled the bases, got around, and there was a big argument with the umpires. Drew Coble was the home-plate umpire and Jim Evans was on the first-base line. He said it was fair, but Tim Welke was at second base and Welke said it was foul. They decided to call it a foul.

"I was ticked off and angry. They made me go back up to bat, and I struck out. I threw my bat, threw my helmet, came back to the bench, and sat down next to Donnie. Donnie started screaming and yelling at Drew Coble. Drew thought it was me, and after the next pitch that was thrown, he pulled off his mask and threw me out of the game. I wasn't even looking. I was totally looking the other way. It was pretty funny."

Wade Boggs

"I probably had more interaction with George [Brett] than I did with Donnie at the time. I really wasn't in a scenario in which I would go to New York [with the Red Sox] and Donnie and I would go out. When I went to Kansas City, George and I would go out. When I got to New York, that's when my relationship with Donnie went through the roof.

"We became really good friends and went out all the time. It was kind of humorous because everyone thought that when I got to New York we were going to butt heads and we wouldn't get along. Quite the contrary, we were best of friends, our families were best of friends, and our kids did sleepovers all the time. In '94, Donnie was the first one to call me at 1:15 in the morning to congratulate me for winning my first Gold Glove.

"I didn't really know Donnie in the mid- to late '80s—just from what he did on the field. Other than the Ted Williams article that we did in '86, I was really never around Donnie. I don't know if it was the New York–Boston thing. I really didn't understand the situation. But when I went to New York, our friendship exploded. It was more of a professional relationship while I was in Boston. We were cordial to each other on the field. He was the best in his town, and I was the best in my town. I had already won two batting titles by '86 and was going for my third one. I always knew going into a season that it was either going to be Donnie or George [Brett] or Rod Carew who was going to be right there. Then later on, Kirby Puckett started showing up and hitting .350."

Don Baylor

"He was a serious baseball player. How can I say it? He had fun off the field but nothing that got in the way of playing baseball, because that's what he wanted to do. He had fun, but he earned being captain of the club. You can't be a clown as a captain of the club. He took it seriously just by the way he played. When you're the captain of the New York Yankees, that's serious stuff."

Jason Giambi

"Donnie was one of my heroes when I was growing up. Everyone knew who Donnie Baseball was. When I first broke into the big leagues, he was still playing. Not only that, but I got to hang out with [Mark] McGwire and got introduced to [Mattingly]. He signed a bat for me, which was an incredible moment for me. Then having the opportunity to go over to the Yankees and have him around at spring training— not only that but have him be one of the coaches, one of the hitting coaches—I really got a sense of why he was so successful. His knowledge of the game is incredible.

"I hurt my knee and had knee surgery in the offseason—I want to say in 2003—and he helped me retool my swing that next year and

the year after that... because he had such knowledge of the game. He was a guy who had a lot of back injuries, so he really had to know the mechanics of the swing to make him successful because his back just wouldn't let him do what he needed to do. He was a huge part of my success after I had the knee surgery, [and he helped] get me back and playing the game. We had a great relationship then and we have a great relationship now. When I see him with the Dodgers, I'll go up and hug him and thank him. We're still good friends today."

"The biggest thing for me is that aura about him. When I was a kid and I idolized him, he had this presence. If you were to draw up a baseball player, I'd say it would be Don Mattingly. Even his mustache was cool. I mean, everything about him [was cool]. He looked great with his glove dangling, the way he wore his uniform. Everything about him represented what you'd call a big-league ballplayer. Then getting to know him, he definitely lived up to that expectation of what [I imagined him to be]. He was a great human being for his knowledge of the game and just how he is as a person."

Andy Hawkins

"Donnie was just a leader. He'd been around so many strong personalities that by the time I caught up to him he was just a leader. It was his turn to lead, and he excelled at it."

"He led vocally, and he led by example. He played hard. I know he had some back problems during the time I was there, but when he was on the field, he was 110 percent physically.

"I didn't get to see him in his real prime, but he was still amazing to watch."

John Wetteland

"He's a consummate pro. He prepared as [well] as anybody. You could see how much passion he had for the game. He truly just loved playing baseball. It's always refreshing to see somebody like that.

"Nothing ever changed him. He was the kind of guy who, when I would introduce him to friends, would treat them like he'd known them for 15 years. He is just a wonderful, wonderful man. A special man. He is revered by his teammates, and rightfully so."

* * *

Mike Pagliarulo likes to talk about how he and his buddy on the other side of the diamond talked about "going to war" every game—especially against certain tough left-handed pitchers.

"One time, we were facing [big lefty] John Candelaria and [Mattingly] said, 'There's only one way to hit this guy, you know that, because he's so deceptive.' I said, 'What's that?' And he said, 'You can't move. You can't pull off the ball. You cannot move. And if you move, he'll get you flinching—that's how he gets all the lefties out, so you can't move.'

"So that day—I'll never forget this—we were in California. We made a promise. We were ready to die that day. I went on deck and said a prayer. I got in the box and I said, 'You watch me, I am not going to move. That ball's coming at my head—ball's coming at me—I'm *not* moving.' He made the same promise. That's how we had to put it: going to war.

"So I went in the box and...I took a stride, and I screamed.... The catcher asked me, 'You all right? That ball was right over the plate.' I didn't move and I said, 'Man, I saw that ball for a long time.'

"Donnie ended up getting two hits that day and I even ended up getting one or two hits off him. That kind of approach was private. It was an approach to get you ready to play and be the best player you could be that day. It wasn't about dying, wasn't about saying prayers, wasn't about the war, it was just about the state of mind that you had to be in. It was total commitment, because there are three elements of performance—the physical, psychological, and spiritual. That spiritual element is the commitment level, and that's what was so private.

"And that private part is what was so cool. Not many people know about it. You could see that…. A guy would take a pitch, and the guys would be on the bench and say, 'Oh shit, watch out.' You'd see that with Manny [Ramirez], see it with Donnie. There were certain guys who you could tell were locked in. There's something about them [that makes you think], *Man, there's something about him today.*

"That total commitment level of 100 percent being there [is] a really hard place to go. And when you're there, you elevate your performance because it aligns [all three elements of performance]. And when they're aligned, you're the best you can be. So we would try to get to the best against the toughest pitcher—that's the only way we could think about doing it. I know it sounds crazy, but afterward, it was like fun."

Mattingly was 5-for-18 lifetime against Candelaria, a onetime teammate and one of several tough left-handers Mattingly was able to hit during his career.

* * *

Don Baylor was a teammate from 1983, when Mattingly truly arrived, through 1985. Baylor then followed a similar path after his playing days.

"Sometimes I'm called Donnie Baseball, and I know he's called Donnie Baseball, too," said Baylor, the Colorado batting coach, before a game at New York's Citi Field during the 2010 season. "I just remember that when he first came up, he could field with anybody—we called him 'McThingly,' 'the Thing'—[because he'd] hit a little *thing* to left field. That was his nickname around the cage. One thing that he really worked on and was successful at [came in] winter ball. He went down to winter ball [thinking] if he's going to play in Yankee Stadium, he's going to learn how to pull the ball. You hit the ball out of left-center field or hit it down the line in Yankee Stadium.

"He came back in '84 and won a batting title, establishing himself as one of the real true threats—home runs, RBIs, big hits late in the game— and the left-handers didn't bother him at all. He was one of those guys who you plug in hitting third for you for 10 years, 12 years. If he didn't have back problems he probably would have won a couple more batting titles.

"I never had a bad back, but I can imagine that trying to hit a baseball with a bad back was no fun at all. Todd Helton's gone through that."

From the other side, Baylor knew what Mattingly was going through once the back went bad. He saw him put limits on a great hitter, who just never stopped.

"He never complained about it. I never saw him back off from anything. As far as being hurt, you never knew because he went out and played. There were no complaints with him. That's why I loved him as a teammate. He was a great teammate."

"He could have played in every era," Baylor said. "You always look at guys [and wonder], *Could he have played in this era? Could he have played in that era?* Yeah, he made himself [into] a power guy. He didn't look it. If you look at his stature—he wasn't a big, Dave Winfield-type guy. He was a line-drive hitter who hit the ball in the air for home runs. He put up some numbers in Yankee Stadium that power hitters who played there did."

Baylor doesn't hesitate when asked if Mattingly is among the great players of his time.

"Without question he was," he said. "You didn't want to see him at the plate. You'd bring in a left-hander, and it didn't bother him. Without a bad back, he would have probably had a run of maybe 10 years or so [during which] he was the one of the best players, one of the top five players in the game."

But Mattingly never made it to baseball's promised land, neither playing in nor winning a World Series.

"Rod Carew was [another] guy who was a great hitter who didn't play on a World Series team," Baylor said. "A lot of [the Yankees'] championships were won after Donnie. He just missed his window there. They had good players, but then other teams had better players at the time. And he was a good player, a *great* player. He did it all."

"He was the type of guy who made solid contact, hit the ball where it was pitched, and didn't try to do anything extra. He took advantage of what the pitcher gave him," said Hall of Famer Jim Rice. "Whatever a pitcher gives you is what you take—and then when he makes a mistake, that's when [the batter] capitalizes.

"He wasn't a follower, he was a leader. You knew that when he came to the ballpark, he was ready to play. I think a lot of people look at his hitting, but he was sweet at first base, also."

* * *

Kirk Gibson's 1984 Tigers romped to the world championship during Mattingly's batting title season. When asked what stands out in his mind about his longtime opponent, Gibson said, "His consistency. When he was the Don Mattingly everybody remembers, he was just a guy who always had great composure, was very much under control, very tough to get out, and played the game the right way.

"He was very consistent—and very dangerous. He had a good understanding of how to approach the game, how to play the game, and he had a very good baseball IQ. When you watch his hitters to this day, I can see a lot of Don Mattingly in them, in the way they foul pitches off and things like that. He knew how to stay alive. He was never an easy out. He always came at you. He always played the game hard until the end."

"Donnie was extremely focused—a very smart hitter, great defensive first baseman," said Marty Barrett, the Red Sox second baseman during those years. "I remember when I had to sacrifice [bunt]. I was really conscious of not only getting it down but getting it down soft enough so [Mattingly] had to come a long way for it so that he wouldn't come down quickly and throw the guy out at second. Hitting-wise, [Mattingly] was really smart, aggressive…. I heard at one point that he always strode for the ball like it was a breaking pitch and then adjusted to the fastball. I don't know if that's what he really did, but I thought, *Wow, that's amazing.*

"He was kind of a quiet guy.... He just calmly went about his job, and whenever you got a base hit and you got to first base, he'd always say hi and ask how things were going."

Barrett had a greater appreciation for Mattingly because neither of them were what you'd call prototypical athletes.

"I think he was an inspiration to somewhat smaller guys like him," Barrett said. "To have the power he did and just how tough he was and how he always would grind it out [was inspiring]. Obviously he was a much higher-caliber player than me, but I thought about it the same way and went about the game the same way.

"It was fortunate for us but unfortunate for the rivalry that the Yankees really weren't that good when I was playing," Barrett said. "They were in one of those lulls. It never really seemed like we were playing an important series against them [that would have] made it memorable."

Barrett recalls Mattingly as a player who never showed anyone up. "He never had a reason for a pitcher to throw at him.... He was a solid guy."

And how do you pitch to Mattingly? "You have to mix it up," Gibson said. "When he was raking, he was raking. You just hoped that he wasn't feeling too well. You had to mix it up.

"He had no [single] major weakness. He had the ability to adjust. If you were going to pound him in, he would adjust on you. He had that short porch there in Yankee Stadium. If you tried to go away, he could go with the ball. He was always a step ahead of you."

"It didn't matter which ballpark [he was in] because he took what the pitcher gave him," Rice said. "[A hitter's] home runs are going to come on mistakes, base hits are going to come on mistakes, but you just hope that when they make mistakes, you have the chance to hit the home run, you have the chance to elevate the ball."

Larry Bowa saw Mattingly play from the other league but coached with him in New York and Los Angeles. Bowa noted that Mattingly's philosophy is to play the game the right way—hard.

"I think sometimes he watches today's games and shakes his head a little bit, because it's about effort, going out there and grinding everything out," Bowa said. "It's about not giving at-bats away. [He] never gave away at-bats. You could see his determination when he got up to the plate. He was an outstanding hitter and great first baseman."

Longtime coach and manager Jackie Moore acknowledges that it couldn't have been easy for Mattingly not to win in New York. "That's why you tip your hat to him," Moore said. "He played the game hard…. I know he was very disappointed in that situation, but in his performance every day, he brought his game to the ballpark. He left nothing on the table."

"Watching that playoff game in Seattle when they got beat—he had never gone to a World Series—you could read the disappointment on his face," Bowa said. "I think a lot of those players wanted to see him go to a World Series because he never had that opportunity and that's something that, as great a player as he was, I think he feels there's a void there. It's not his fault, obviously. It's the people you play with. But I think when he watches World Series games, he's probably saying, 'That would have been nice.'"

It didn't taint what Mattingly did during his playing days—not in the eyes of those who Mattingly played or coached with or against.

"First time I ever saw him was in Double A," offered Phillies manager Charlie Manuel, a baseball lifer who has found roaring success in the Philadelphia dugout (after, by the way, the *experts* predicted the same doom they're predicting for Mattingly in L.A.). "He was at Nashville, and he had a parallel stance at the plate, just slightly closed, and he had a really quick bat. He was a tremendous hitter. I followed him when he came to the major leagues, when he came to the Yankees.

"He was what I call a 'prototype hitter.' He had a high average, he could hit for power…. He wasn't a guy who would try to hit home runs…. If you go ask him, he might not tell you he was a home run hitter, but what he did was he consistently hit the ball hard, hit line drives, and when he got the ball up in the air he'd homer.

"He was one of the guys in the big leagues I used to love to watch because he had a short, quick swing, and everything about him was geared for baseball. He was that good. I used to talk to him every now and then when he was a player with the Yankees—not a whole lot, [but] I'd have a conversation with him. I always loved watching him.

"He used the whole field and basically would take what the pitcher gave him. He hit the ball a lot where it was pitched, but he also knew how to hook the hole when a guy was on first base.

"Obviously he was a very tough hitter. It's too bad he had the back problem. I know what that's like. He is obviously a classy guy."

"He was *good*. He was one of the best defensive players as a first baseman in the game at that time," said former catcher Tony Peña. "He saved so many games defensively, it was unbelievable. Sometimes in baseball you only see…the offensive numbers. Sometimes you forget about defense and how many games a player can win for you defensively. But he was a great defensive player and also a great offensive player."

And there was another thing one observed, according to Peña: "The love and the passion that he had for the game and the way he went at it."

"In every game you saw Don Mattingly play, you saw the same guy every day," said Texas Rangers manager Ron Washington, who played against Mattingly in the mid-1980s. "He never changed. He's a great guy and great human being, but he also knows baseball.

"One thing I always remember about Don [was that] he beat you in so many ways. I think everybody knows what he could do with the bat, but I think sometimes they took what he did defensively—what he did with his intelligence on the field—for granted. He was a winner. Now he's over there in L.A. with those young hitters, and he's turning those guys into winners."

Washington, who played against Mattingly with the Twins, Orioles, and Indians, recalls pregame meetings in which the teams would discuss the Yankees hitters.

"In those meetings, you'd say, 'If Don Mattingly comes up in a situation, we can't beat him,'" he remembered. "If the score dictates that we can walk him, try to see if you can get him to chase something. And don't take anything for granted when it's thrown to first base because most of the time he'll come up with it. Don't get relaxed over there at first base because he'll put on a back-door pick.

"He definitely had command of the strike zone. He was a quality hitter. What did he hit, nine home runs in a row? That tells you something right there. That's pretty tough to do."

* * *

Veteran announcer John Sterling is never one to be shy with an opinion. Starting back when he was a brash sports talk show host in New York, Sterling has always said what he feels.

"Don Mattingly is the most beloved player I've ever seen in New York," Sterling stated.

Sterling said later, "I can't imagine Don Mattingly ever getting booed. I've seen every other player, at some point or another, get booed...but Mattingly transcended all of that.

"I'm not sure I understand *all* the reasons why. He was beloved by the other players, and it somehow spread to the fans. I guess they recognized a guy who cared nothing about the publicity, sublimated his ego, played hard all the time, and played well. You can say the same thing about Derek Jeter, and maybe someday I'll say that about Jeter when he finishes his career. But of all the players that I've seen—it doesn't matter whether it's basketball, baseball, hockey, or football—I felt as if Mattingly had connected with his fans better than anyone."

Yes, even Jeter has been booed. A slow start one year had the folks in the Bronx on his case. Yet no one can remember Mattingly getting the same treatment.

"It's easy to cheer someone when they're hitting .340 with 25 homers and 120 RBIs, but if you're not hitting home runs and your batting average gets down to .250 or something, whatever happened in the end for Donnie, I never heard him booed," Sterling said. "I mean, he's just *loved*—purely, completely loved.

"You know what the test would be? The test would be if he ever becomes the manager of the Yankees and the team loses. I heard Willis Reed booed when he was coaching [the Knicks]. Everyone gets booed when they're the coach or manager, so that's the only reservation I have."

Suzyn Waldman, Sterling's sidekick, offered a possible reason for the special relationship between Mattingly and the fans. "I never heard him booed," Waldman said. "There's only one other athlete who I never heard booed at Yankee Stadium, and that was Bernie Williams. There is a quality that the two of them share, but Mattingly is very different. I think he is the most loved—I'm saying loved, very different than being respected and all those kinds of things that a DiMaggio had. I think it's Donnie's warmth that came through everything that he did.

"There's something that Don Mattingly has always had—everybody liked him. He was everybody's son, everybody's brother, everybody's friend. He just had that way about him.… Of course it goes with the fact that he was a great player and he made it look easy, but we knew he worked hard. If he had a great catch of a foul ball, the ball went up in the seats. He [gave the ball to] a little kid who was sitting in the front row and [he ate popcorn from the kid's bag]. That was Don Mattingly, the little grin after that and he took some popcorn out of the kid's bag and ate it."

Waldman recalled the night Mattingly got his 2,000th career hit—on the road.

"He got it in Anaheim, and when I tell you [about it], you would have thought you were in Yankee Stadium when they put it up on the board. I'm not kidding," she said. "It was universal. Nobody ever booed Don Mattingly—ever, at any place. I don't even think they booed him in Boston."

The crowd at the Big A that night stood and cheered a player for the visiting team. Now, perhaps West Coast folks tend to be more laid back and don't treat the opposition rudely, but this was above and beyond. That night, those people recognized something special.

"I think he was the perfect Yankee," Waldman said. "He never did anything wrong, but there was a warmth there. There was something that everyone could relate to. I don't how you can relate to a lot of these guys now, if you're a kid.

"He was a living testament to work ethic.... Obviously he had great talent, but there are a lot of baseball players that you look at and you say, 'I could never do that.' But there was something about Mattingly that made you think, *You know, if I had worked a little harder, or if I had done this, maybe I wouldn't have had to do this. Maybe I wouldn't have had to go work in my father's bank.*

"There was something about Donnie that was so endearing.... I sort of compare him to Dustin Hoffman on the screen, because you look at Hoffman on the screen and you think, *I can do that.* Well you can't, but he makes you identify with him. [Mattingly made players believe,] *If I had just worked on my swing, if I had just worked on my footwork at first base...* Well, you couldn't have.

"There was a warmth and an endearing quality that came out of him all the time that I think people just jumped on. Also, you got the feeling that he tried. No matter what it was, he tried. Even if he [made] out, he was never booed because he was trying as hard as he could—all the time. I think that goes a long way in fans' minds.

"His whole essence is just so working class. You could sit down and have coffee with him. You could go out and have a beer. You know, there are a lot of people [in baseball] you wouldn't bring home to dinner."

The writers, who obviously have their ups and downs with everyone they cover, felt it, too.

"I love the guy," said Michael Kay, who covered Mattingly first for the *New York Post* and then as a broadcaster on the YES Network. "I absolutely love the guy.

"He's probably the most likable and my favorite person I've ever covered. He just seemed like a guy who was going to work. He didn't make it seem like he was above everybody else. We were writers, we were broadcasters, and his job was [to be a] baseball player and he didn't think he was any better than you. You almost felt he could be wearing overalls and going to work—he had that same attitude. He just seemed like he was happy to be there, worked his butt off, didn't really complain—not that we knew of. He treated everybody with respect. He was a total joy. You wish that everybody you cover was like that."

"[He has always been] the same dude," Kay said. "I covered him in the last couple of years, when he was a supernova star, and then with the back injury,

Don Mattingly faced a rapid-fire series of questions from host Michael Kay on the YES Network's *CenterStage* in 2003. His answers were:

Favorite movie: *The Negotiator*
Favorite song: "Long Time Gone" by the Dixie Chicks
Favorite musician: John Cougar Mellencamp
Favorite food: New York pizza
Favorite athlete: Michael Jordan
Favorite baseball player: "Jeet" (Derek Jeter)
Favorite sport to watch: basketball
Favorite sport to play: golf ("Are you good?" Kay asked. Answer: "No.")
Favorite city: New York City
Favorite city besides New York: Seattle
Favorite book: The Bible
Favorite actress: Sandra Bullock
Favorite actor: Samuel L. Jackson
Favorite television show: CNN's *The Morning Show*
Favorite moment: Coming onto the Yankee Stadium field for the first time during the playoffs in '95

and there was no difference. There was no bitterness when the back robbed him of greatness. ... He's the kind of guy who, if you had a son who became a baseball player, you would want him to turn out like Don Mattingly."

Sterling recalled Mattingly's popularity. "I joined the Yankees in '89. People asked to get his autograph. In the clubhouse, we would be lined up, and I'd be in a line with seven or eight players. *Everyone* got Don Mattingly's autograph on something. He wasn't a hardass about it—he did it gladly and willingly. He was such a good guy. There would be a line all the time. This was in the clubhouse, this wasn't on the field."

Sterling added, "He had tremendous abilities. It's too bad his career was cut short by the bad back, because he was the kind of hitter who could hit .330, with power every year. And he was a *great* first baseman. And he was a great leader."

* * *

Mickey Hatcher won't ever forget the other tourist he met on vacation.

"I was in Aruba with my wife and we were doing an excursion, a Jeep tour," said Hatcher, now the Angels batting coach. "I kept telling my wife, 'That guy over there looks familiar.' I said, 'I know him.' He had a hat on, so it didn't click. [We got to a] stop and he was in the other Jeep. He got off and said, 'Are you Mickey Hatcher?' I said, 'Yeah,' and he said, 'I'm Don Mattingly.'

"It was funny that both of us happened to be in Aruba at the same time. I think it was the first time that I really got a chance to sit down and talk to him. There was the hitting coach for the Dodgers and the hitting coach for the Angels, we were both in Aruba having a Freeway Series. We ended up getting on the same Jeep and we spent the day together, and I really got to respect him a lot. He knows a lot about the game—and he's a bigger guy [physically] than I thought.

Hatcher had a nice playing career, hitting .280 during 12 seasons with the Twins and Dodgers—but he was *not* Don Mattingly, one of the bigger names in the game. Yet it was Mattingly who recognized Hatcher and initiated the conversation. That's Mattingly.

"It was great," Hatcher said. "We spent that day together. I knew he had the opportunity to get that Dodgers job once Joe Torre got out of there. And after getting to know him, I know he's going to be a great manager in the game [because of] the knowledge that he had talking baseball, talking what he's gone through and where he's been.... I played for Minnesota, and there wasn't much pressure there.... When you play with the Yankees and put up the numbers there...there's always pressure for those guys in Yankee Stadium. There are fans who always expected that from him. There was a higher standard for baseball at that time, [something] we're trying to create here with our guys. It goes to show you he did it, and he did it with the Yankees."

Michael Kay recalled a story related to his transition from print to broadcast media, another sign of what kind of a guy Mattingly is.

"I got the radio job after the '91 season, so my first year was '92," Kay said. "I think it became official that I got the job sometime in January. Donnie and I were close as a ballplayer and writer, but we never called each other. He didn't have my number or anything like that.

"It was a January morning when the phone rang in my house, and an operator was there, saying, 'A person-to-person call from Don Mattingly.' I said, 'Yeah, sure,' and it was him and [then-wife] Kim on the line. They were in Hawaii on vacation. I said, 'What's up? What's wrong?'

'Nothing—we just heard that you became the announcer, and we're so proud of you. We think it's so great, and we just wanted to take the time to call and congratulate you because you've always been so fair with us and you've always been such a good writer and a good reporter. This is just so great, and I know this is something that you always dreamed about, and we're really happy.'

"I mean, what other ballplayer does that? I said, 'How'd you get my number? You're in Hawaii.' He said, 'I have my ways.'

Kay, who calls Mattingly "the one shining light in a dark tunnel," was with the Yankees for much of Mattingly's time in New York. And during that time, he only saw the other side of Mattingly once when he was covering the Yankees for print.

"I was a writer, and I guess I wrote something about him that wasn't too complimentary," Kay said. "There was a whole crowd of people at that corner locker, and I was the only guy who wrote this. He was looking out toward me but not *at* me, looking out over the whole crowd. I was on the outskirts of it. And he said something like, 'Yeah, and those *assholes* write some stuff that's just not true.' It was totally un-Mattingly-like.

"So I was steaming, but I let it go and he ran out on the field. I was leaving the ballpark that night and Kim was outside. I was always close with Kim, too. I said hello really brusquely and then walked away. She grabbed my arm and said, 'What's wrong with you?' I said, 'Your husband's an *ass*.' She goes, 'Why?' and I told her and she said, 'Oh, he's not that.' I said, 'Just leave it alone.'

"So the next day, I walked into the clubhouse and he called me over. I guess Kim aired him out. 'I'm really sorry I said what I said. I shouldn't have said that. You've always been really good to me, and if you wrote something I didn't like I should never have said that.' So then I pushed it. I said, 'Well, that's all well and good, Donnie, but you embarrassed me in front of 25 people and you're apologizing to me alone. Apologize to me in front of everybody.' He said, 'Don't push it,' and he smiled and walked away."

Bob Schaefer, who managed Mattingly in Greensboro in 1980, remembered, "I had a buddy in Connecticut who was going to open up a satellite TV store. He was a big Yankees fan, and he knew Donnie. He said, 'If you bring Donnie up here to sign autographs, I'll give you a satellite and give him one.' I said, 'Sounds good to me,' because satellite TV was a big thing at that time.

"By the time I called him he had gotten the MVP award, so that made it even better. He came up and I said, 'Donnie, you have to come up for the weekend and we have to go down and sign some autographs.' He said, 'No problem.' So he went down there and the guy gave me a satellite. Unfortunately, Donnie lived in New Jersey and they had zoning there, so he couldn't put up a satellite on his land. He never got the satellite.

"He never said, 'Thanks a lot, I did that for nothing.' He just said, 'That's the way it goes.' He's always been a guy who appreciates where he is, and he got there because of his work habits and his personality. He's a special guy in the history of baseball, no doubt about it."

And with all of his success, Mattingly never really stopped being a kid who just loved to play the game. That's not a negative. He was a smart, savvy star who exceeded so many forecasts of what he was going to be. But even in 2010, as he was approaching his 50th birthday and his first season as a manager, there is a little kid in him that still comes through. Okay, it's a battle-worn little kid, but he hasn't changed that much.

Waldman recalled another example of that from Mattingly's playing days: a meeting Mattingly had with a star of a different sport, another star from Indiana.

"He was a big Celtics fan—and he could do Johnny Most," she said, talking about the famed Celtics announcer with the raspy voice. "Don Mattingly did the best Johnny Most of anybody I've ever heard. One year we were in Fort Lauderdale. Larry wife's last name was Mattingly—no relation—and the Celtics were in Miami. Donnie wanted to go meet Larry Bird. Donnie and the kids went down and out came Bird with a basketball.... Mattingly was *nervous*. And of course Larry's not the greatest talker in the whole world. They met and they made small talk and Larry had a ball and Larry started bouncing the ball, I believe it was to Preston [Mattingly's son]. As the kids were throwing the ball back and forth to Larry Bird, the conversation got a lot warmer.

"It was great to watch. He wanted to meet him."

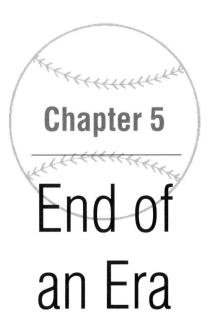

Chapter 5

End of
an Era

"The reason I quit playing was because when I went home to my house in New Jersey, when [the Yankees] were at home, I felt like I was at a hotel."

—Don Mattingly

The 1995 season was extremely difficult for Don Mattingly and was in fact his last. His back was in need of constant work and, to make matters worse, his kids were back in Evansville much of the time. That meant even home games seemed like road games.

"I always looked at the reason I quit playing as that," Mattingly said of wanting to be with his kids. "That's the reason I quit playing. It wasn't because of my back. It wasn't because I got nicked up…but the reason I quit playing was because when I went home to my house in New Jersey, when [the Yankees] were at home, I felt like I was at a hotel.

"I would go from my house to the ballpark. I'd come home and I'd go up to the bedroom, and I'd come back down, maybe swim or something in the morning to get loose, and I'd go back to the ballpark. And I kept finding myself getting to the ballpark earlier and earlier. If I was on the road I'd go to the hotel, go out and have some drinks or whatever, hang out with the boys some, then go back to the ballpark. [In New York,] if your family's there, you spend time at home—then you get a little normal life, you get a little real life. *Then* you go back and you do what you love to do."

It seems like if you asked 100 people why 1995 was Mattingly's last year, 50 would say it was his back and 50 would say it was his family. But for Mattingly, the reason was clear.

Regardless, there still was work to be done in 1995, and the Yankees, coming off a labor-shortened season that saw them leading the American League East by 6½ games with a 70–43 record when things shut down, should have been ready from the start to make that last push. If the players felt it was the last chance for Mattingly—and there were indications that it was—they should have been killing themselves out of the gate.

They started off well enough with a three-game winning streak and seven wins in the first nine games. But they fell to 16–25 by June 12 and were 26–31 at the end of June. A 17–11 July made things respectable, but an eight-game losing streak in August dropped the mark to 53–58. They split the next two to sit at 54–59 on August 28. At that point they turned things around, closing the season on a 25–6 run, including a 22–6 mark in September and October, to clinch the wild card on the final day of the season.

According to Mattingly, "We got to a point where we just started talking. It was like, 'We have to win every night.' There was a big number there down the stretch."

The Yankees won an impressive 18 of their last 22 games to get to the playoffs. Once they clinched, Mattingly got down on the turf of the SkyDome in Toronto and let loose a fist pump that showed the world what it felt like to finally make it to the postseason.

Mattingly, speaking on his *Yankeeography* years later, said, "I'd heard so much stuff and played the most games without getting in the postseason.... It kind of puts a mark on you, like you're the reason that they're not getting to the postseason. So to get there was a good feeling, to get that little monkey off my back."

The Yankees celebration that day was more than that of just a team that had clinched a playoff spot. Those guys wanted to get there for their captain, and they'd made it. They believed they should have made it the year before, but a strong finish earned them a date with the Seattle Mariners.

Mattingly had done more than just gone along for the ride. From September 9 he went 24-for-74 for a .324 batting average and 10 RBIs. He hit safely in the final 10 games—at a .371 clip—including a home run off Pat Hentgen in the finale. He singled off Mike Timlin in what would be his final regular-season at-bat.

"That last little run we had at the end of the season in '95 just to make the playoffs—I mean, that was fun baseball," said teammate Paul O'Neill. "Looking back, it wasn't like it was a pressure situation. It was fun, because we were in a situation that the Yankees hadn't made the playoffs in a long time. I remember that well, and I remember we won a lot of games down the stretch in the last 10–15 days."

Everyone in the clubhouse knew it wasn't easy for the captain to drag himself out there. But he played every single day.

"Yeah, because it was important," O'Neill said. "And it was a fun time to be out on the field because, when you have to continually win at the end, it [felt] like if we won we were going to get there. I think we had a game or two lead or something like that. It wasn't like we were chasing somebody, so we could take care of it ourselves—and that's a great situation. It's a great position to be in on a team that's playing well, which we were."

Said broadcaster Michael Kay, "Yankees fans rooted for the Yankees to get to the playoffs, but *everybody* was rooting for Don Mattingly to get to the playoffs. It wasn't so much that the Yankees hadn't been there in 14 years, it was that Don Mattingly had never, ever been there.

"It was like hanging the Mona Lisa in a garage—more people should have seen it. I'd never seen [such] universal joy. I think even around baseball…because everybody felt that [getting to the playoffs] was just his rightful place, [considering] his skill level."

* * *

The first two games of the first American League Division Series were two Yankees wins that featured some Don Mattingly events no witnesses will ever forget.

The first took place long before the first pitch of the series. Mattingly came out to do his running before the game, and Yankee Stadium went crazy. Their hero had made it to the postseason, and they were going to turn this into a party. There were signs all over the place—"Batman Forever," "We Love NY No. 23," and many others.

"Then when [PA announcer] Bob Sheppard introduced him, the place was up for grabs," said Michael Kay, a Yankees broadcaster. "And then when he hit the home run…I think that was in Game 2…forget about it. I can't remember that place [ever being so] loud. Even after that—[during] the World Series in '96, '98, '99, 2000, '01—nothing was as loud as that. Nothing was as loud as when Mattingly came out. Nothing was as loud as when he hit that home run. It was unbelievable. I got goose bumps.… It was an entire stadium of 56,000 people pulling for one guy.

"Everybody thought they had a little bit of ownership in Don Mattingly. His success made everybody feel better."

Mattingly indeed homered in Game 2 of the Series and the Yankees put themselves the position of having to win just one game in Seattle to advance to the ALCS against the Cleveland Indians.

Both the Yankees and the Mariners had to get sizzling hot down the stretch, just to get there. The Yankees clinched on the final day of the regular season, and the Mariners, once 12½ games out, beat the Angels behind Randy Johnson in a one-game playoff. The ALDS series was a five-game slugfest. The teams combined for 68 runs and 113 hits, including 22 home runs (11 by each team). The Mariners hit .315 against the Yankees pitching.

Games 3 and 4 were rough, but Game 5 marked the end of Don Mattingly's career.

A young Bernie Williams hit .429 with two homers, and Paul O'Neill hit .333 with three home runs for the Yankees. But the Mariners' Edgar

Martinez, whose double would win the thing, batted .571 with two homers and 10 RBIs. Ken Griffey Jr. hit five homers and batted .391, ex-Yankee Jay Buhner batted .458 with a homer, and Tino Martinez, who would replace Mattingly in a matter of months, batted .409 with a homer.

That Tino Martinez signed as a free agent with the Yankees after driving in 111 runs in the regular season was just one of the weird connections these teams would have in this series. For another, Lou Piniella was the Seattle manager at the time.

"Every single game in Yankee Stadium and [the Seattle Kingdome] was close," Tino Martinez said on his *Yankeeography*. "There were come-from-behind wins. There were dramatic home runs."

"It was a great series," Mattingly said, looking back. "It was a fun series to play in because there were some great games in there.

"It was kind of the coming-out party for Mariano because he pitched out of the pen and he was lights out. Nobody touched him. Coney pitched that last game, and he was typical Coney—he gave you everything he's got. He's tough."

But neither pitcher had enough to get the Yankees past a Seattle team that seemed to be a team of destiny—at the time, anyway.

* * *

Don Mattingly didn't announce his retirement after that painful end to the season. But he did tell the Yankees organization he wasn't coming back. At age 34, he was done.

Lou Gehrig was just shy of his 36th birthday when he retired because of a disease that would soon kill him. Mickey Mantle made it to 37 but was a shell of himself the last four years of his career because of crippling knee injuries.

The combination of his back injuries—which now, just 15 years later, might not have been quite so bad with today's training techniques—and his desire to be with his three sons made the decision for Mattingly. He was done.

117

A Look at the First Four Games of the 1995 ALDS:

Game 1, New York, October 3

The Yankees got the jump in the series with a 9–6 win. David Cone earned the win and reliever Jeff Nelson, who would become an important part of future Yankees championship teams, took the loss. Mattingly lined a single to right field in his long awaited first postseason at-bat and went 2-for-4 with an RBI.

Wade Boggs and Ruben Sierra both homered to offset a pair from Griffey, as the young superstar began a power-filled personal show.

Game 2, New York, October 4

The Yankees made it 2–0 when Jim Leyritz dropped a two-run homer just into the short porch in right field in the 15th inning, good for a 7–5 New York win. Mattingly went 3-for-6 and hit one of four Yankees homers in the game. It came in the sixth inning to snap a 2–2 tie.

"The fans want a dinger out of him," Gary Thorne said on television. Mattingly swung and crushed the ball, with Thorne yelling, "Oh, hang on to the roof," as the place went nuts.

Young pitcher Mariano Rivera made his postseason debut and got the win, coming out of the bullpen in the twelfth inning, pitching 3^{1}/$_3$ innings of two-hit relief, and striking out five. No one knew then, but it was the start of what would become one of the great postseason résumés of all time.

"I think I pretty much knew I was going to retire," he said recently. "I didn't officially retire then because I didn't want to retire and [months later want] to play again and come back. I thought I was done at that point, though. I kind of knew by the second half of that year, really.

"At that point, obviously I was disappointed. We had a 2–0 lead in that series, we had a lead in [Game 5], and then we had a lead in extra innings.... Cleveland would have been next, and I thought we had a legitimate shot at beating those guys. We played them well all year long [6–6, as opposed to

Game 3, Seattle, October 6

The Mariners stayed alive with a 7–4 win behind Randy Johnson, a pitcher who Mattingly had owned during regular-season play. Johnson fanned the Yankees captain three times in Mattingly's 0-for-4 effort.

Mike Stanley and Bernie Williams (twice) homered for the Yanks. But Johnson beat Jack McDowell, something he would do again in Game 5, when both came on in relief in the finale. Tino Martinez homered to seal the victory for the M's.

Game 4, Seattle, October 7

The Kingdome was rocking again when the Mariners scored five runs in the eighth to beat the Yankees 11–8. Yankees closer John Wetteland failed to retire any of the four men he faced. One of them, Edgar Martinez, hit his second home run of the game in the inning.

The Yankees scored two in the ninth, but it wasn't enough to overcome their deficit. They were now facing a one-game playoff to advance to the ALCS—and try to extend Mattingly's career.

Mattingly was 4-for-5 including a two-run single in the first inning of the penultimate game of his career.

4–9 against Seattle]. It's probably like anything else—it was just kind of a sudden ending. Cora bunt, base hit, it's over. A base hit and a double down the line and it was over. … It was sudden, but in a sense it really felt like that was it."

Asked if he was okay with that, Mattingly said, "Oh yeah, I was okay, really. That was a tough series to swallow because it was one of those series [before which] a lot of energy went into that season. For me it starts back when we had those bad teams. For a couple of years, Mr. Steinbrenner was out of baseball and we were a bad team. When Showalter came over, we started coming out of it. We started getting the right kind of guys again.

"You could see the light. I felt proud of that because I felt I'd been on good teams, in '85 and '86, with Winfield and all those guys. They were great teams. Then we went through a period of two or three years there when it was really bad. It was like we weren't even competitive."

Mattingly, Buck Showalter, and better decisions by the front office (and fewer by Steinbrenner) helped bring the Yankees back to the cusp of what would happen in 1996.

The loss to the Mariners was the end of two upbeat seasons for the franchise. The Yankees were 70–43 and leading the AL East when the labor dispute ended 1994, and then the team shook off a bad start in 1995 to become the first American League wild card team with an impressive rush at the end. It was a much better way for the proud career of Mattingly to end.

"The year, '94, we had the lead when the strike hit," he said. "We felt like, *Man, we have a four- or five-game lead when the strike comes. We're going to get in the playoffs.* I felt like we were going to get in the playoffs. We had a good team. We had a good chemistry going. Guys played hard together. Guys could just feel it. It was fun.

"It really brought me back because it was fun for me and I could just feel the energy. It overshadowed [the back trouble] a little bit and it overcame those bad years. It stinks being on bad teams at the beginning of the year. You battle it and you battle it, you know you can't give in to it, but being on a team late in the year when you have no chance…it just stinks.

"So in '94, [the strike] happened and then '95 we were not playing that great. Then as the year went on, it was the first year of the wild card so we felt like we were in that hunt. We got to a point where we just started talking. We said, 'We have to win every night.' And I don't know how many we won down the stretch, [but] there was a big number there down the stretch. So all of that was a kind of culmination. And I knew that it was probably going to be it for me, so it all kind of slammed right then [when Griffey scored]."

"I think a lot of great players want to know how they would do in big situations," O'Neill said, "and I think [Mattingly] answered that question in the '95 playoffs. He was able to play in that playoff and played really well. That was a really big thing. We didn't win it that year, but getting to the playoffs and knowing that he competed well in the playoffs was very important to him. And as disappointing as that was for the team, the way we lost in Seattle, I think it put a good ending on his career, knowing that he did that well in the playoff situation."

And it all occurred while Mattingly was in a lot of pain. "It was a struggle [for Mattingly]," Wade Boggs said. "Toward the end he didn't like sitting there…he went on the disabled list a couple of times, then came back and did the rehab. He was so used to playing 157 and 159 games a year…that once he got into the 80, 90 [range] and struggled and had to work out more—because he wasn't getting the playing time because of the bad back—it just caught up with him.

"We were all upset that they pulled the plug on us in '94, because that was probably one of the best Yankees teams that I had ever been associated with. That would have been Donnie's first playoff, and we would have gone to the World Series without a doubt. That was another stake in Donnie: not going to the playoffs and not getting the recognition in the postseason that he well deserved.

"We were just in shock, because it happened *so* quickly. We kind of felt that since we were two-up with Seattle, all our cards were pretty much in line. All we had to do was go out there and win one game. Come one, just win one game out in Seattle! Then they wound up winning three, and we were just stunned. It was more shock than anything.

"Donnie wasn't there in '96, but I think that fueled a lot of fire for us in '96 to say, 'We can't let this happen again,' because we had been through it. It was just so sad for Donnie. [Had we won] one game against Seattle then, boom, here we go—we're on our way."

Said closer John Wetteland, "It's one thing to ask your body for one more night, one more night, and…then when it's done your body gets a chance to say, 'Okay, now tend to me.' When you look at the prospects of another entire year, that's quite a bit different. You could see it on [Mattingly's] face, too. Man, I mean it was rough. He knew. I remember sitting in the Seattle clubhouse after we had lost. I saw him a few times, and I could just see it in his face. He knew that was it, that was his last chance. It was pretty hard to look at it.

"He left it all out there, and that's a wonderful feeling. He'll always be able to look in the mirror and say, 'You know what? I left every little bit out there. I didn't hold back a day.' As a professional, that's all anyone can ask of you."

"We were in the training room in Seattle, crying," Boggs remembered. "He had told me that this is it. I said, 'Cap, how can this be it—you just wound up hitting .417 in the playoffs.' He said, 'No, I'm done.' I said, 'you've got to be kidding me.' We're sitting in the training room and he says, 'No, I'm not coming back.' I said, 'Well, just take a month, a couple months off in the offseason and don't rush to judgment or anything like that.' He said, 'No, I'm done.' He was very adamant about that. We wound up winning in '96 and I think that sort of crushed him because '95 was the first year that he had ever gone to the playoffs and he had a wonderful playoffs. You just sit there and go, 'Man, all he had to do was just come back for one more year and everything's perfect.'"

Showalter knew there would be no change in Mattingly's thinking. The manager said, "We got through with the last game in Seattle, and Donnie basically said, 'Listen, I can no longer do, over the course of the season, what the first baseman for the New York Yankees needs to do physically. I just want to give you guys a heads up, going into the off-season.' [He told us] he was basically not coming back, that he was done. He just wasn't going to play the game like that and put us in that position.

"It's very sad to talk about it because I knew he wasn't going to be able to play, but the impact he'd had on all those young kids still carries over to today. Paul O'Neill still talks about it today. O'Neill came in as a kind of hot-head...but you could see the way he adored Donnie.

"[Mattingly] could have continued to play, but I think he knew his back, he knew the pain he had gone through. It's not that he wasn't willing to make that sacrifice anymore, but he wasn't sure the Yankees were going to get the return that they needed. He had some challenges at home with his family. He wanted to be there for his boys. How many guys would have had the guts to make that decision? It's something, obviously, that he had thought about, but even then he was thinking about the welfare of the team and not waiting until February of the next year. That's when we went out and got Tino Martinez because we knew far enough in advance.

"[Mattingly] stood up during the whole trip back from Seattle, because he couldn't sit down with his back."

Trainer Gene Monahan knew how tough it was for Mattingly to play every day.

"[He would go through] two, three weeks at a time when he would have a problem. He had to come very early and do a lot of whirlpool baths and a lot of stretching, a lot of spine stabilization work that he learned very well from Dr. [Robert] Watkins' group out in L.A.," said Monahan, who is now closing in on 40 years as the Yankees' trainer. "He had to do this every day and then at home as well.

"He worked around the clock...but it took him about an hour and a half every day just to get moving. And some days, it just wouldn't crank and he would play at less than half of what he had, mobility-wise. Some days he couldn't go at all.

"He had some degenerative disc problems. They may grow as one gets older, obviously, and obviously now and later on they are going to be arthritic. It's a tough deal. With the rotation [of batting] and pushing off, it was very tough for him, even on defense."

Monahan said it was even tougher for Mattingly because he generated his batting power out of his legs and lower half. "Donnie obviously hit a tremendous amount for average, but I remember the time he hit those homers eight days in a row and then got all those grand slams. He used his legs better than anybody I've ever seen. From the waist down, when he would rotate and push off his back hip—his left hip—he had such power and torque.... That really saved him. That really helped him and it kept him hitting. But when it got so bad to where he couldn't turn, he had to try to flip that ball to left field and he was getting a lot of base hits from center field over toward left, [and] that wasn't Donnie."

It was too much of an ordeal for him to play a 162-game schedule.

"You can [compare it to] an NFL player who's into his mid- to late-thirties, trying to get to training camp," the trainer said. "Spring training was such a tough deal for [Mattingly] and such a tough price for him pay—though he didn't mind doing it because he loved the game so much.... Finally it got to the point where all the work that was successful and got him to where he was started to take its toll. He just became tired. Those muscles serving that area became weak instead of getting stronger because of all the work he had to do to artificially get going.... It just finally took its toll on him, and he finally said, 'That's enough.' There's no question that yes he could've played another four or five years, easily [had it not been for the back]."

That's why the first baseman got the message to the Yankees that he wasn't coming back.

"They kind of knew," Mattingly said. "There were conversations back and forth after the season was over. I knew—[but] I didn't want to make a decision right then. I wanted to hopefully get a little bit of time. But I also knew that they needed to do things. Once the season is over you have to figure it out. I couldn't just sit there and hold them up.

"I knew the position that they were in [and the one] that I was in. I told my agent right away that I wasn't going to mess around with it. It just got to the point where I just said, 'Hey, Jim [Krivacs], let them know that I'm not going to play.'

"They were trying to hold off for me. I told Jim, 'Let them know. They have to go do what they have to do.'"

So they went out and got Tino Martinez, who would be the first baseman on four world championships in the next five seasons.

And Don Mattingly faded off into the sunset. "It was coming, yeah," he said. "Obviously, [I would have liked] the chance to win it all. I remember seeing a sign at Yankee Stadium sometime during those years that said, 'Don Mattingly, the Chosen One,' and I thought to myself, *Chosen for what?* He laughed. "You know what? It's funny. Obviously I'd like to have rings, would have loved to have had a chance to have gotten some and loved to have been on a team that won it all and be a part of that…. I could have kept playing. I was still swinging the bat, I was fairly healthy, I was having little problems, but I was fairly healthy. A lot of people say, 'You got out because of your back.' I got out because my kids were at home and they hardly came to New York anymore.

"They were starting Little League, and I was leaving for spring training. I'd see them now and then, and I knew if I stayed I wasn't going to see those guys grow up. It was really a pretty simple decision. When I look at it like that, I look back and say, 'You know what? I wouldn't trade those years that I stopped [playing].' I saw [my kids] grow up. I got to go to the Pony League World Series with my oldest one. I went to another division of that World Series in Omaha with Preston. I traveled to all these baseball tournaments and basketball tournaments [with them]. We traveled and stayed at the Motel 8, went to five games a day…. You can't trade that."

The decision to retire was not a forgone conclusion, though.

"I was going back and forth," Mattingly recalled. "I never got tired of playing. I loved the challenge of playing. I loved the challenge of getting ready to play. I loved being around the guys in the locker room. It was such a fun time. I never got tired of that. Most people have the misconception [that I quit because of my back]. I quit playing because I wanted to see my boys grow up."

* * *

Don Mattingly did most of his damage as a hitter in the final era before performance-enhancing drugs. He played the second half of his career with a bad back that may well have been helped by such chemicals. Like Hall of Famer Mike Schmidt, Mattingly admits that he doesn't know what he would have done if the opportunity to use steroids had presented itself.

Schmidt, who battled back and shoulder troubles, said in 2005, "Thank God steroids weren't available to us in the '70s and '80s. I, and many who will remain unnamed, would have been 40 pounds heavier trying to keep up with the Joneses—especially since the combination of leading the league in home runs and becoming a free agent meant millions. ...

"If I had played in the 1990s, I would have used steroids. Why? Because I'm human."

He eventually backed off his original statement, but the message was clear. And he's not the only former player to have said basically the same thing.

"I'm there, too," Mattingly said. "Honestly, [when] you compete, and you see some guy over there just crushing balls and you're battling back injuries [for all] those years, you never know what you would do. And that's being honest. I just can't say.

"When you're that [young], you think, *Hey, I'm bulletproof. I'll just do a little bit.* You hear maybe it's bad for you, but you just think, *Oh, you know.*

"I'm with Schmitty on that. I'm glad I didn't have to make that decision. I'm really proud of the fact that I never was part of that, though. I know that the 145 [RBIs in 1985] I put up was all natural. ... I put up 238 hits [in 1986]. All the things I did were straight up."

Mattingly hopes things are changing for the better. "I'm glad there's testing," he added. "I hope testing gets to the point where no one can get away with anything."

Much of the steroid era took place after Mattingly was out of the game.

"I was out for eight years before I even came back to the field," Mattingly said. "I was around baseball a little bit and saw some of the [increased home run production] and I was amazed.

"To be honest with you, I didn't watch that much baseball early on.... I would watch the playoffs, because that's what interested me. I was [always] interested in how guys played in the playoffs. Down the stretch, last two weeks, and then into the playoffs, I always wanted to see who was really doing well then.

"So I didn't really pay that much attention. I didn't really realize how big guys were. Then I came to a playoff game. I remember seeing guys [and thinking], *Oh my God*, because they were huge. I just thought, *Man, these guys are just big guys.*

"People would ask me at home—there was a little talk about it—and I'd say, 'There aren't that many guys doing it. There just can't be that many guys doing it.' I think I was naïve about that."

* * *

Mattingly went home for the 1996 season. He had opened a sports bar, Mattingly's 23, but quickly decided to get out of that business because he "didn't want to sit around and talk about the old days." He was home, he had his farm, he was with his family, and he didn't have to prepare several hours a day to get his battered body ready to play a baseball game or get on a plane to fly somewhere else to play baseball.

Meanwhile, Wade Boggs and others spent the 1996 season waiting for Don Mattingly to walk through the door.

"We expected to see him in spring training," Boggs said. "He had told me in the training room, 'This is it, *boom*, I'm not coming back.' Then the offseason went by and we were getting ready for spring training. We heard Don Mattingly had announced his retirement, he was not coming back because of a bad back, and he was not going to spring training. ... He never came back to spring training, he never came back to Yankee Stadium. It was like he just rode off into the sunset and the sun went down—and that was basically it."

He just drifted away. Throughout the year, there were rumors about [Mattingly joining] Cleveland, Baltimore, and St. Louis—but Boggs recalled hearing other things.

"We heard that his back was doing better…he was going to make a comeback and sign with another team. I said, 'That'll never happen. If he comes back, he'll be back in New York.'

"But all the reports were that he was doing fine and he felt fine. [Trainers] Gene Monahan and Steve Donahue were sitting there saying, 'Hey, I talked to Donnie.' He called the stadium and Geno said, 'Oh, he's doing well, his back's responding.' He was doing some treatment with some trainer and it was [working]. We all thought, *Wow, is he going to come back? Be on our roster? Maybe he can come back and he and Tino [Martinez] can switch off, play first and DH, DH and first.…* But it was just all silly rumors, I guess."

Mattingly stayed away from the game—completely. He was on his farm in Evansville, playing with his kids, doing real family stuff. It was tough for him to watch baseball; it was easy for him to be with his kids.

His teammates, on their way to the franchise's first world championship in almost 20 years, missed their captain.

You could even say that they won it for him.

"Absolutely," said closer John Wetteland, who threw the final pitch of the 1996 World Series. "We actually talked about it. He's a Yankees great, period. Even during that season we would talk about him here and there, saying, 'Gosh, I wish Cap was doing this with us.'

"We actually left his locker the way it was. Nobody was allowed to go in there. We still had his nameplate up there."

Jim Leyritz, who idolized Mattingly, said the sudden end to the 1995 season, with the Mariners winning three straight, denied the Yankees and Mattingly any real closure.

"It was tough because when we left after we beat Seattle in Game 2, after I hit that home run, we thought we were coming back," Leyritz said. "We never felt like it was Donnie's last game. It was kind of like Paul O'Neill and the sendoff that he got [in 2001]. It was such a great thing, everyone knowing it was probably going to be his last game. Donnie never got that—and that was one of the regrets that I had about losing to Seattle that year. We just didn't finish it off, number one. And number two, we never gave Donnie his farewell that he deserved.

"Don't get me wrong—a couple years later [the Yankees] had a day for him, but it still wasn't the same thing."

"I think he had a lot to do with that team, really, because '95 was really the start of '96. And '94 also. [They were all] winning seasons," Paul O'Neill said.

Said Bernie Williams, one of the young guys Mattingly helped usher into the big leagues and who had become so important to the team, "[There were] mixed feelings. We wanted Cap to be there to enjoy the time because we knew that he was certainly part of the team."

While the Yankees were winning their 23rd championship—the first of four in a five-year span—Mattingly was at home with his family.

It was natural that he felt left out, especially since he never got that World Series chance. He was comfortable in knowing he had finally made it to the postseason and done well there, but the first Yankees World Series since the year before he broke into the major leagues went on without him.

"To be honest, it just didn't seem right doing it without Don Mattingly," general manager Brian Cashman said on *Yankeeography*. "Nothing really seemed normal, actually, in 1996 without Don Mattingly."

As it turned out, it was the only year Mattingly was completely away from the game.

Many former Yankees greats joined the team as special spring training instructors. They all seemed to come back, and that's what Mattingly did in 1997 when he began his return to baseball and came back to the only team he ever played for.

* * *

Replacing a legend is never easy in any walk of life. Replacing Don Mattingly in New York was even harder.

"I knew what I was getting into," Tino Martinez said of signing with the team as a free agent when Mattingly retired. "I knew the fans loved Donnie."

Martinez had helped hasten the end of Mattingly's playing career when he batted .409 with a homer and 5 RBIs in the five-game ALDS series that brought down the curtain on Mattingly. Eligible for salary arbitration, the Mariners couldn't afford to keep Martinez and he was traded to the Yankees in December. He then signed a five-year deal with an option for a sixth season—way above what Martinez would have accepted considering the Yankees trained in Tampa, his hometown.

"Tino and I had been friends—through [agent] Jim [Krivacs] to start with," Mattingly said. "He told me about Tino coming [to New York]. Tino actually bought my place in Jersey."

Martinez batted .293 with 31 homers and 111 RBIs in 1995. He then faced the toughest challenge of his life.

It didn't go well at first. "I remember calling Tino. He struggled early on," Mattingly said. "He was having trouble in New York. Anybody who came in there [would have had trouble]. It's not as if they don't like the guy coming in. I think it's respect for the guy who left. You didn't want to be the guy who came after Nettles, like Toby. Toby Harrah came in after Nettles and just got *crushed*. And they did the same thing to [Jason] Giambi once Tino left.

"It's respect for the guy who played before you—you have to show them. I knew Tino, how hard he was on himself and how tough he was. I knew he was a great player. I remember talking to him. I said, 'Tino, just keep going, man. Just keep playing, do your thing, be yourself. You're going to be fine.' And he had a great year. He just had a slow start. Sure, it was tough on him, but he just kind of rolled on.

"We were friends," Mattingly said. "And I had a lot of respect for him, the way he played. ... I definitely wasn't snubbed by the Yankees. They were always great. Mr. Steinbrenner was always great."

Martinez had been a hero in Seattle the previous year but the Mariners couldn't afford to keep him. Being from Tampa, the Yankees' spring training base, and knowing the Yankees needed a first baseman, Martinez wanted to go to New York. He said he would have jumped at a two- or three-year offer, but when the Yankees offered five with an option for six, it was a slam dunk.

"I knew what I was getting into. I knew the fans loved Donnie," Martinez said on his *Yankeeography*.

"It's pretty remarkable as you look back because Donnie Baseball is an icon. Nobody wanted to follow him," David Cone said on the same show.

"I always had the utmost respect for him," Martinez said.

Said baseball writer Jack O'Connell, who covered the team at the time, "From the beginning, Tino let Yankees fans know, 'You guys love Don Mattingly and I do, too, and I respect him. I'm not trying to replace him. I'm just trying to succeed.'"

A May 1 extra-inning grand slam in Baltimore turned Yankee Stadium boos into cheers. The next night Martinez took off. He wound up driving in 117 runs (that season), and even a poor postseason couldn't dampen the fact he had endured a very tough situation.

"There was no more Mattingly hangover," O'Connell said. "I think fans were very happy to have Tino Martinez on that field."

Added fellow writer Bill Madden, "I think the fans appreciated that [Tino] came into [a] very difficult situation, and he didn't let them down."

Martinez wore No. 23 in Seattle but wore No. 24 for the Yankees. Speaking about his jersey number change in his own *Yankeeography*, Martinez said, "I personally feel that [Mattingly] should be the last guy to wear that number. I don't want to be the guy who wears it and all of a sudden they retire it."

Martinez played in five World Series with the Yankees, five more than the man he replaced. He was one of the most popular players on a team of Yankees superstars.

He was not Don Mattingly, and that was just the way he liked it.

* * *

It came as a surprise to no one that Don Mattingly officially retired in January 1997. But he did return for the spring training visit and was there on Opening Day to help Joe Torre and New York mayor Rudy Giuliani raise the 1996 world championship banner.

It wasn't the only honor for Mattingly at Yankee Stadium that season.

On August 31, 1997, Don Mattingly became the 14th player to have his Yankees jersey retired. He was enshrined in Monument Park during a moving 40-minute show of love for "Cap," one of the great Yankees of all time.

"That plaque in center field means more to me than you'll ever know," Mattingly said years later.

But the day itself was a strange one for Mattingly, who still has a what-am-I-doing-there attitude more than a decade later.

"I like that—a lot," he said. "I never even imagined something like [that happening]. I came there a Punch and Judy [hitter], didn't hit the ball anywhere, and DiMaggio and Mantle and Yogi and those guys [came before me] and now [I'm] out there [in Monument Park] with *them*?

"How'd that happen? I don't know how I got out there," he said with a laugh. "I don't know... seriously. I just kept playing."

It happened because Don Mattingly is one of the Yankees greats. He was a captain and a leader.

"It's a good feeling, honestly," he said. "You look at the organization, the history.... When I came to New York, I had no clue of the history of baseball. Even the book I'm reading now about Jackie Robinson—stuff like that you learn over time.

"So it's pretty special when people consider you one of those guys. I don't take it too seriously.... I just went out and played and did the best I could, and [that's] what happened. It's one of those things that came from getting ready to play, playing hard every day, absolutely wanting to be the best I could be, and this is how I got there.

"I don't know how it happened, but I just kept playing—and honestly, tried to treat people right along the way. I tried to treat people with respect.

My father always said to treat people with respect. Obviously you have to play and put up numbers, but if you treat people wrong along the way you don't get the respect back. If you treat people right, I think you get respect from that. If people don't want to treat you right back, then okay, but you still treated them right. That's how I always went about it.

"When [my number was retired], I felt like I was still a kid. I was 36 years old. I thought, *What am I doing out there with these guys? Mickey Mantle and Babe Ruth*! ...I started thinking about my life. I grew up playing in high school in a fairly small town in Indiana, and then I was in New York and *there*. [The reason] it happened was that I just went out and played.... It's simple, right?"

The day was obviously special, complete with gifts for Mattingly and his family. ("A ridiculous kind of day," he said). But there was one thing, something that happened away from the ceremony, that still stands out in Mattingly's mind.

"My little one [Jordon] was really little," he said. "He was something like five [years old]. He wanted Cracker Jacks and kept bugging George, 'Where are those Cracker Jacks?' George said, 'You are going to be successful because you are persistent.' And [Steinbrenner said], 'Get somebody to get him some Cracker Jacks.'"

It's rather typical of Mattingly that he would have a day like this—to have gifts including a ring, a car, and a truck lavished on him, and to get a plaque in Monument Park—and 13 years later remember the interaction between his son and George Steinbrenner.

And it was also rather typical behavior from Steinbrenner.

"He was great. We were up in his office, and he was great," Mattingly said. "He was great pretty much 99 percent of the time to me.... I'm sure when I didn't get hits or didn't get a run in he was mad—but other than that one little period of time there, he treated me great.

"He always made me feel like I was part of the family. He was always larger than life. He was the Boss, he was larger than life, and he had that thing about him, but he was good with me. He was great with me."

The Record on Donnie Baseball

Now more than a decade later, the records section of the Yankees media guide has Mattingly fourth all time on the club in doubles (442); seventh in both at-bats (7,003) and hits (2,153); ninth in games (1,785); 10th in batting average (.307), runs (1,007), and RBIs (since 1920, 1,099); and 11th in home runs (222).

Other notables in the book:

- He had a club-record 238 hits in 1986.
- He smacked a team-record 53 doubles in 1986.
- His 24-game hitting streak in 1984 is the eighth best in Yankees history.
- He was the American League MVP and RBI champion in 1985.
- He was the 1984 American League batting champion.
- He hit a major league record six grand slams in 1987, a mark matched by Travis Hafner in 2006.
- He matched Dale Long's big-league record with a homer in eight straight games in 1987 and set a record with 10 homers in the eight straight.
- He was a six-time All-Star.
- He came up wearing No. 46 but in 1984 became the 28th and last Yankee to wear No. 23, a number worn by Tony Lazzeri, Luis Tiant, Don Zimmer—and Ralph Terry when he served up Bill Mazeroski's World Series–winning home run in 1960.

The wording on Mattingly's plaque read, "A humble man of grace and dignity. A captain who led by example. Proud of the Pinstripe tradition. And dedicated to the pursuit of excellence. A Yankee forever."

* * *

When Don Mattingly retired as a player, he watched his sons play baseball and noticed that young baseball players were having trouble holding the bat properly. He wound up developing a bat with "V-Grip" technology, and a company was born.

Go to www.Mattinglybaseball.com, and you will find a video of Don Mattingly discussing his product.

The company made news during the 2010 Little League World Series by sending a shipment of the bats to the Fairfield team playing in Williamsport, Pennsylvania.

Mattingly called the kids before the game. "I encourage you guys to have fun today," he told them. "Congratulations on getting there. I have been watching, [and] it has been fun being able to follow you guys." He told them the big-league eyes were watching.

"You would be surprised how many guys love watching [Little League] games," he told them. "I think it's that when guys are playing, they love to see you guys play because you have so much fun and it takes us back to when we were kids."

On the charitable side of things, he created Mattingly Baseball Charities, working with business manager Ray Schulte.

"Mattingly Baseball Charities has been formed to try to help inner-city baseball," Mattingly said. "Inner-city baseball has been one of the [things] that I saw more of when I got away from playing and I was back at home.

"Watching my boys play and traveling [and] playing in tournaments we were here and there. It wasn't just a sample of Evansville. It was everywhere we went. I didn't see hardly any inner-city kids playing—and you have to get baseball early in the inner city. The kids don't get started [because] they don't have the money, they don't have the facilities to get started.

"I did some stuff out here [in Los Angeles], donated some of the Dodgers' equipment to fields and gyms. We [helped] a field back at home [in Evansville] through the Boys & Girls Clubs and helped to generate some money for Harlem RBI.... I wanted to form this Mattingly Baseball Charities because that's been one of the areas that I wanted to be able to touch. That's how it started, and that's what we're doing."

The mission statement on the organization's website reads:

Mattingly Baseball Charities has been created to serve underprivileged youth by supporting programs which promote baseball and softball participation in conjunction with other developmentally related activities. Mattingly Charities will provide funding and services and equipment for baseball, softball, and ultimately other sports, and related youth development activities, for the benefit of underprivileged youth, youth leagues, and social welfare and related organizations. 100 percent of the efforts of the organization will be focused on these activities.

Initially, Mattingly Charities will partner with existing charities that already have established operations and aligned mission statements and serve primarily as a source of funding and equipment for these organizations. Funding will be generated year round through various activities, including special events and direct solicitation of the general public. The activities above will be conducted by paid subcontractors or employees.

* * *

Today, Mattingly's coaching philosophy is the same basic principle that propelled him into Monument Park:

"I really go back to the idea that things need to be simple. It really comes down to taking care of your business on the field. Take care of your business on the field, and that's your main priority—outside of your family. You say, 'Okay, this is my job, this is what I do, this is what I love to do, this is what I'm taking care of.' It's not, 'Am I getting into this party? Am I on a billboard? Who wants to do a commercial?' It should be, 'This is what I love to do, this is what I know *how* to do.'

"I try to tell…our young guys [with the Dodgers], 'Go out, play to win, get your four good at-bats a night, every night. Every night, four at-bats, four at-bats, four at-bats, four at-bats, concentrate every night. At the end there's a pile of numbers lying there, and that's what you are at that point.

"But it all comes from basically bearing down and keeping it simple, giving yourself four chances to get hits and hitting four balls hard every night. That's only one part of the game, though. Then there's another part: it's about playing defense. And then there's another part: you have to run the bases, and you have to know [when].

"There's a whole game that's being played there. [Many people] think [statistics] come from the offense. Very rarely do people talk about what kind of base runner a guy is—unless he's Rickey [Henderson] or a guy who steals a ton of bases like Juan Pierre. How many times do you talk about [Paul] Molitor and say, 'Do you realize what kind of base runner he was?' [Molitor] and [Robin] Yount were a nightmare on the bases. Both of those guys knew how to play, how to run the bases. They got the best jumps. If you had those guys on first and third, you could not throw through because they're going to score. It's like Little League stuff—you couldn't stop those two. They would score on balls and you'd think, *Man, these guys are the best base runners I've ever seen.*

"But no one talked about that, really. I knew that as a player, and I saw that as a player, but would [a reporter] write that? Fans aren't necessarily interested in it [either], but to me that's what greatness is about—guys who are all that."

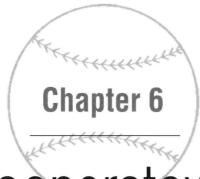

Chapter 6

Cooperstown Controversy

"Why is Sandy Koufax in the Hall of Fame today? I know what I think. A lot of [Koufax's] stuff was [based] on what would have been. If you're going to start going there, Mattingly's a first-ballot guy."

—**Buck Showalter**

S andy Koufax was 129–47 during a glorious six-year run with the Dodgers that started in 1961 and ended with his premature retirement in 1966 due to elbow trouble. He was 97–27 his last four years and is generally regarded as the best pitcher most people have ever seen. His record before that run was 36–40.

Yet Koufax was a slam-dunk Hall of Famer, getting 86.9 percent of the vote from the Baseball Writers Association of America in 1972, his first year on the ballot. The honor was well deserved.

A decade after Koufax's election, Don Mattingly was on a marvelous six-year run during which many were calling him the best player in the game. A bad back then cut down Mattingly's numbers and eventually knocked him out of the game.

Mattingly hasn't gotten a sniff of the Hall. Yet many think he belongs.

"You better believe it," said broadcaster Ken Harrelson. "Koufax [is] a Pedro Martinez. Sandy wasn't any better than Pedro for a five- or six-year period. Pedro was as good as there was for a five- or six-year period. And Mattingly was as good as there was for a five- or six-year period.

"And if you take the total package, name somebody better. I'm talking about defensively, too. [Mattingly] wasn't just a good defensive player—he was an *outstanding* defensive player. He was a great first baseman. So you put those together with the window he had. I don't care if he makes it or not, but to me he'll always be a Hall of Famer—and I'm pretty selective about who I'd put in there.... He'll always be a Hall of Famer to me because of all the positive things and no negatives."

The voters clearly don't think so. The voters love longevity, the cumulative numbers that populate the back of a player's baseball card. There are now voters with ballots who have never seen Mattingly play. It doesn't help that his career was cut short.

"Like Koufax, he didn't have the longevity...and he threw up some gaudy numbers," Don Baylor offered.

"It's a shame that he hurt his back," Larry Bowa said. "I think he would have had a great shot at being in the Hall of Fame."

Said Bob Schaefer, "He doesn't have the longevity [voters] are looking for, but at the time he was the best player in the game. To me, he's a Hall of Fame person and a Hall of Fame player.... Hall of Famers are guys who dominated the sport when they played, so for that factor I'd say he is a Hall of Famer. But unfortunately, because of the injuries, he didn't play as long as he should have played."

One can tell that the Hall would have been a nice cherry on top of a well-baked cake for Mattingly, but he treats it with his usual shrug.

"I don't really worry about it because, in the end, it doesn't change anything for me," he said. "Status-wise, I guess it puts you in a [certain] category.... I can look back very easily and wonder, *If I could have played just another five years and been healthy...what could have happened?* But that's just what if.

"I'm sure there are a lot of guys in that category, guys who got hurt [who would] have had long careers. They'd have been right there, maybe. It doesn't change the way I feel about myself.

"After the first year or two [of voting, I was] curious to see what would happen. I didn't think in any way, shape, or form that I was going to get voted in, but I was curious to see what it would look like…. Now it gets really disturbing when you see the kind of numbers that you put up and then see the kind of numbers during this era we've been in. Those numbers [make mine look] pale."

Looking at Jim Rice's long-awaited enshrinement, Mattingly said, "[It's] unbelievable. He should have made it before that. Even Andre Dawson and Goose [Gossage] took [too] long. Bert Blyleven was really close this year. He'll be in, but he was a great pitcher. What separated him [from 300 wins]? Ten wins or something? It's an artificial number. I just know that he was damn good."

Mattingly earned 28.2 percent of the vote in 2001, his first year on the ballot, and that's the closest he's ever come to the necessary 75 percent. His vote dropped in each of the next four years and strangely fluctuated from 15.8 to 11.9 to 16.1 percent over the three seasons leading up to 2010.

When asked if Mattingly should join him in the Hall of Fame, Jim Rice said, "I'd have to say yes. When you look at a guy who you can start a ballclub with, a guy who can lead a ballclub, a guy who plays every day and sets examples, he's that type of guy."

Texas manager Ron Washington, an infielder who played against Mattingly, said that Mattingly is a Hall of Famer in his mind. He knows

Don Mattingly's Percentages of the Vote from the Baseball Writers' Hall of Fame Ballots (75% needed for election):

2001—28.2%	2005—11.4%	2009—11.9%
2002—20.3%	2006—12.3%	2010—16.1%
2003—13.7%	2007—9.9%	
2004—12.8%	2008—15.8%	

about the shortage of numbers and his longevity and remarked, "I think that probably may come into play, but [he is] a guy who impacted the game in the years that he played it—he certainly impacted it."

Jack Curry, a voter who previously worked for the *New York Times* and is now with the YES Network, *doesn't* vote for Mattingly.

"I can't answer for everyone, but I will say that I have a Hall of Fame vote and I give him serious consideration," Curry said. "But to me, even though you mention other players—Koufax being one that everybody latches onto—I think that the numbers fall off so dramatically.... I just think for me that those six years weren't enough to elevate him to Hall of Fame status. I just think that, for me, he fell a little short.

"I know a lot of Yankees fans bring up the [Kirby] Puckett comparison and how close their numbers were. It did surprise me, to be honest with you, even though I didn't vote for him, that his totals have been so low, that his percentage has been so low. I thought he'd get stronger support."

Said colleague Michael Kay, who left the writers' side for the broadcast booth and thus doesn't have a vote, "They say you're supposed to be objective, but I would have been clouded by my [fandom].... I was a fan of [Mattingly] before I even became a writer. I would have judged him on the personal level, too. I always compare his stats to Kirby Puckett. They're pretty comparable. I think I would have given him way more consideration than he's gotten—that's the best way I'll put it."

It is interesting that both Kay and Curry brought up the Puckett comparison. In *Out by a Step: The 100 Best Players Not In the Hall of Fame*, a book coauthored by this scribe and Neil Shalin, the Puckett comparison is a major part of the chapter on Mattingly.

Ian Browne, then of Sportsline.com and now the Red Sox beat writer for MLB.com, wrote that after Puckett made it on the first ballot and Mattingly wasn't even close the same year, "They played in an almost identical number of games—1,785 for Mattingly, 1,783 for Puckett. Puckett hit .318 and had 2,304 hits, compared to .307 and 2,153 for Mattingly. Mattingly had 222 homers, Puckett had 207, Mattingly drove in 1,099 runs, Puckett 1,085. Mattingly won nine Gold Gloves while Puckett had six.

"Both retired following the 1995 season and [2001] was their first time on the ballot. So it's fair to ask why Puckett got 423 votes and Mattingly finished with a paltry 145, 242 votes shy of the 387 necessary for enshrinement."

Puckett, of course, led the Twins to a pair of World Series titles, while Mattingly only appeared in the postseason once.

"I think they're two of the best players in the league and they should add another player to [the Hall], but Mattingly's going to be there for what he did for Yankee Stadium…and the type of hitter he was," predicted Mickey Hatcher, a teammate of Puckett's. "There's no telling what other kinds of numbers he could have put up, because I know the last few years, when I was playing, he really had the back problems going. I think it kept him from having huge numbers. He was just the type of guy who, if I was watching a game and he came up to bat, I would stop to watch him hit."

"Without the back thing, [he is] certainly a Hall of Famer," said Lou Piniella, Mattingly's former teammate, batting coach, and manager. "First of all, look at his defensive prowess: he was excellent around first base, with great hands, excellent range, and could turn a double play. He threw from the left side as well as anybody. I would say that in the period Mattingly played, he played first base as well as anybody.

"He was a legitimate .300 hitter, a legitimate RBI guy, a legitimate home run hitter, Gold Glove–type first baseman. You take away the back injury from Donnie and [if he had played] another five or six years in top shape, [he would have had] Hall of Fame numbers."

Said Puckett, who passed away in 2006 and was, like Mattingly, an ambassador of the game they loved to play, "I idolized Donnie. Like me, he was the first person there and the last to leave [the park]. The only difference between Donnie and [me was that] I went to ten All-Star Games in a row. Donnie went to several. But the Yankees [never won] the World Series. I won two [in five years]. That may have been the thing that put me over the top. Other than that, we were pretty much the same type of ballplayer. I know that we both played hard every day."

Buck Showalter said, "Why is Sandy Koufax in the Hall of Fame today? I know what I think. A lot of [Koufax's] stuff was [based] on what would have been. If you're going to start going there, Mattingly's a first-ballot guy."

"For a stretch there, there was probably not a better hitter than Donnie," said Hall of Famer Wade Boggs. "He consistently drove in all the runs, and his power numbers went up, and [he won] Gold Gloves every year. So when you talk about one of the premier players of all time, he's right there. It's just the back situation. That he didn't get to play another three or four years to add some stuff onto his legacy is probably the reason he's just never gotten any consideration for the Hall of Fame."

"The type of body that he had and the kind of athlete that he was, he could easily have played until he was 40, 41 years old," said Tom Grieve, who tried to acquire Mattingly in a trade when Grieve was the general manager of the Texas Rangers. "[Considering] the hand-eye coordination that he had, he wouldn't have been hanging on. He could have still been a very productive guy late into his career. His career shut down because of that injury right in the prime of his career.

"Look...what is A-Rod going to do after he's 30 years old? I'm not saying Mattingly would have put up those kinds of numbers but he would stayed a .300 hitter until he was 38 or 39 years old, easily."

Mattingly won't dwell on the what-ifs. "It is what it is, and I played my cards. And I think you always look back as a player and say, 'I could have done this,' and, 'I wish I would have kept hitting more than people told me,' [but] I'm proud of what I did. I think more than anything I'm proud of the way I played the game and how I cared about it. I got myself ready to play. I mean, that's the biggest thing—I came to play every day. I didn't really want to sit out. I didn't like taking days off.

In *Out by a Step,* former Mattingly teammate Willie Randolph said, "He was as good as any I've ever seen for that period of time. He was in one of those zones. He had a great supporting cast around him. Donnie had a great situation. He was in a beautiful spot. It always amazed me, as much as he was raking back then, they still would pitch to him rather than pitch to Dave Winfield. I always thought that was weird. You have to respect Winfield, too—he's a Hall of Famer—but it just seems that sometimes Donnie was a tougher out than Winfield at certain times. But they would continue to go after him, and he would continue to rake."

"If you go by a body of work over a six- or seven-year period, he was clearly one of the elite players during that time frame," Flanagan said. "The back injury really hampered him, but he was as good as there was for a six- or seven-year period.

Kirk Gibson said he played with a couple of pretty fair infielders in Detroit who would fall into the Mattingly Hall of Fame category.

"There's so many people that I played against [for whom] you could make an argument for them to be in the Hall of Fame, and there are many who argue he should be or he shouldn't be," Gibson said. "Alan Trammell and Lou Whitaker are guys who I played with that come to my mind. I don't even get into those discussions. If [Mattingly's] fortunate enough to get in, I'll congratulate him. If not, he still had a great career, he was a great player, and he is well-respected in the way he approached it."

Asked about Mattingly and the Hall, broadcaster John Sterling, who didn't join the Yankees until 1989, just before Mattingly's offensive path was headed downward, said, "You're asking the wrong person. First of all, I think he was a Hall of Famer, and I would vote for him tomorrow. He's everything you could want in a ballplayer—a teammate, leader, captain, he's everything you'd want—so I would vote for him."

Unfortunately for Mattingly, Sterling doesn't have a vote.

Added Tony Peña, who played against Mattingly and later coached with him, "To me he is [a Hall of Famer]. There are a lot of players who never had a chance to go into the Hall of Fame. Some players deserve to be there and some others, maybe not. I think [he does because of] what he did for this organization and what he did in baseball. It's too bad his career was shortened because of his back problem. There's no question that if he would have continued to play he would have had huge numbers.

"I think, to me, he's a Hall of Famer. There's no question he was a great first baseman and a great hitter."

* * *

Mattingly's not in the Hall, but that doesn't mean he's not represented. Following is a list of Mattingly items in Cooperstown:

- The bat used by Mattingly to hit his sixth grand slam home run of the 1987 season on September 29 off of Bruce Hurst of Red Sox at Yankee Stadium—a major league record for most grand slam home runs in a season.
- A bat used by Mattingly during his 1986 season.
- The bat used by Mattingly on July 18, 1987, when he homered off of Jose Guzman at Texas, the eighth-straight game in which he homered, tying Dale Long's major league record.
- A first baseman's mitt used by Mattingly during his career. Mattingly retired with the highest fielding percentage of any position player in history and was a nine-time Gold Glove winner.

Mattingly has a friend in charge of the Hall. President Jeff Idelson was the Yankees' public relations man from 1989–93.

"What made Mattingly stand out above others was that he fully understood the responsibility of being a baseball player beyond the diamond," Idelson said. "He always understood the importance of meeting with [others], whether it was the underprivileged or ill or one of our sponsors. He understood that was part of the responsibility that came with being a major league player.

"He's also one of the few guys I know who had a great deal of fun when he played, [although] he took it seriously. I don't think I ever saw a better first baseman…. George Scott was pretty good, but Mattingly just stood a class above [him] because of the way he handled himself."

If you've ever seen Mattingly speak, you get the feeling he's not the most naturally chatty person you'll ever come across. But he always knew what he had to do.

"He did. He was a quiet leader, kind of like Andre Dawson," Idelson added. "He was a captain in a different way. He wasn't a rah-rah guy, but he led by example. He had strong character, great integrity—and those are adjectives I'd use to describe Andre Dawson in terms of being a quiet leader, someone who set an example that others would follow."

Chapter 7

Back in Uniform

"He's good. He knows guys' swings, he knows their routines. He knows when a guy is a little off, the things the guy is doing that are preventing him from hitting. In studying everyone's swing, he'll know something to say or point out to get [the hitter] back on the right track."

—Casey Blake, Dodgers infielder

It was George Steinbrenner who wanted Don Mattingly to be the Yankees batting coach—not a spring training instructor but the team's batting coach.

It happened in 2004. Mattingly, who had been serving as one of those big-name spring training instructors, took the job. In 2006 he replaced Lee Mazzilli as the Yankees bench coach, and in 2008, after taking some time off to deal with family issues, Mattingly replaced Mike Easler as the batting coach of the Los Angeles Dodgers. Joe Torre felt Mattingly could help the team more in that position, and also pick up the pointers he needs to become a major league manager.

There probably isn't anyone in baseball who knows more about hitting than Mattingly. Always a student of the game, he worked harder than anyone to continue to succeed, even with a protruding disc in his back slowing him down.

The first thing Mattingly learned about being a hitting coach was *not* to try to make everyone a clone of himself.

"I don't think you can do replicas, that's for dang sure," Mattingly said. "Rick Down [the batting coach he replaced in New York] was a good hitting guy. I was around and I remember him saying, 'There are a lot of ways to skin a cat.' A guy may start with his hands up, may start with them down, [his stance] may be open, it may be closed—[but] certain absolutes have be happening at the right time.

"I always [approach] it like I want to study a guy's swing, see how it works. He's had success, he's here. The last thing you want to do is take a young kid who's in the big leagues and say, 'You have to do this.' That's the last thing you want to do. I want to help a guy understand how his swing works so that he can teach himself, more than anything. You want to take that swing, see how it works, and let them [develop] an understanding. Approach has so much to do with understanding what the guy can do on the mound—what he can do and what he cannot do.

"The video is so good now that if you don't have an approach when you walk up there, you're not going to be as good a hitter as you should be, plain and simple.... In the old days you had to talk to everybody— What's his ball doing?—figure out how he pitched you. But now I can go watch this guy against every left-hander or every right-hander or every little guy that he faces, and [learn] how he commands his breaking ball, how he commands the fastball. I know what he can do and can't do. I still haven't seen that last little bit of movement. It's different off the video, and [when] you get up there you're going to see something different. It's going to be late movement, so you encourage these guys to talk [to each other]."

While we know there have been hitting coaches—particularly ones from the Charley Lau school who preach the "cloning" to which Mattingly referred—Mattingly figured the best thing to do was work with what hitters already have rather than trying to make them into something they're not just because that was his way.

"He's helped all of us, I think," said Dodgers center fielder Matt Kemp. "He's one of the best hitting coaches I've had. I've had some good ones, but he's one of the best. The main thing with him is he doesn't try to teach you to hit the way he hits; he teaches you your strengths. He teaches you to stay with your strengths. He has a lot of knowledge for the game and he knows what he's talking about."

He also teaches his hitters to play the game the right way. That's something Mattingly *doesn't* mind cloning.

"Everybody remembers [him as] a guy who always had great composure, was very much under control, very tough to get out, and played the game the right way," said Kirk Gibson, who was the Arizona Diamondbacks' bench coach before taking over as the manager soon after speaking these words.

"There's never a day goes by that he's not in the batting cage with somebody, trying to help him," said former Dodgers third base coach Larry Bowa, who was also with Mattingly and Torre in New York. "I'm talking about two, three hours before the game. Then they go on the field, and he does all that work. He studies film. I think the biggest thing is he tries to incorporate their swing [into] what he wants to do with them. He doesn't try to change anybody.

"His philosophy is, 'You have be comfortable, and if I tell you to stand a certain way and you're not comfortable, it's not going to work.' I think that's really good, because a lot of hitting instructors say, 'Okay, let's do this. Let's change this.' Donnie's not like that. He wants a guy to be in a comfort zone so [no change feels drastic]. But he also states to these guys that this is a game of adjustments. You can't keep doing the same thing because there's so much film [on] hitters now. They can pick up somebody's defects just like that—what they can't do and what they can do—so you have to stay on top of it.

"Especially with this generation and with our team, we have guys who have a good week and then they don't want to work as hard. Donnie's philosophy is, 'Hey, you work hard whether you get three hits one night or you're 0-for-4.' Methodically, just keep playing, grinding it out. Don't get too high, don't get too low.

"He's making an impact, there's no question," Bowa continued. "Some of them want to go their own way and I think that frustrates Donnie a little bit, but he sticks to the program. He has a lot of them understanding his philosophy. There are just a few who want to do it their way, and the ones who want to do it their way aren't very successful.

"I think Donnie likes to pass along what was passed along to him. If you're a good coach, what you want to do is pass along the knowledge that you got from other people to these guys. Then maybe when they get done they'll coach and they'll pass it on too.... I think Donnie is so much into hitting that it's almost like a science to him."

Mattingly enjoys working with the young guys. "It's been so much fun out here, because in New York it [felt like there were so many] old guys who knew what they were doing and really you're just helping them with their maintenance," he said.

"But here, these guys really don't know what they're doing. They're just up there hitting and they're talented. That's where you start building. 'Okay, why are you swinging at the first pitch that's on the outside corner and down when this guy throws 96? Why? I don't care if it's a strike. Why? What are you going to do with it? We're going to give this guy something here, or take this away. He doesn't throw strikes out there, so why are you looking out there? Why are you going to cover that? Don't cover something you don't have to, or this guy's a sinkerball pitcher, where are we going to look? Where are we going to try and go with this guy?' That part is fun."

Mattingly did not have what one would call a conventional hitting style. It certainly wouldn't be one you'd go out of your way to teach a young player.

"I was kind of down and crouched, a little bit George Brett-ish at times," he said. "That was one of the things I think I changed too much—especially after I got hurt. I really started trying to figure out a way to regenerate. But there are no absolutes—there's no *one* way to hit.

"Obviously, there have been guys over a long period of time in this game who were great [but unconventional] hitters. Carl Yastrzemski—are you going to teach some kid to [hold his bat straight up in the air]? Jim Rice is different, and Boggs is different. Gwynn's different. I'm different. George

Brett, Carew, Molitor—[all of us] are different. Each guy is going to have a little different swing, so you have to help them take what they do swing and perfect it. Are there little tweaks that you try to make along the way to improve it a little bit? Yeah. But you're not making huge changes in guys."

Andre Ethier was born April 10, 1982, the start of the baseball season that saw Mattingly take his first step into the major leagues. Now, Ethier is a kid with all kinds of ability, and he's one of several young Dodgers working under Mattingly, the batting coach.

"It's unbelievable," Ethier said. "Donnie was...done in baseball a little too early for me to key in and see him, but I definitely remember him when I was younger. Even then, as a developing young guy, I remember coaches and people comparing his swing and approach to mine and looking at him as a guy to emulate in [one's] career.

"To get a chance to play under his tutelage is something special. I don't think you realize how great of a player he really is and the numbers he put up. I didn't realize it until I got a chance to go to old Yankee Stadium and see him out there [on] that monument in center field. You realize there are not too many guys out there. I walked through [Monument Park] and saw the plaques they have up and the other names [on them]. You definitely know those other plaques and names, and then to see Donnie mixed in with them is pretty special to see.

"You're going to take a lot from any hitting coach, but he's such a good coach, first of all, without those credentials and everything he's done. But when he puts those behind him, you definitely know he's been there, he's done that. He knows the feelings of the struggles and everything that [a player goes] through on an everyday basis. So you take it a little bit more to heart when he says, 'I know what it feels like,' when he comes at you with something, because you know he's probably experienced it in his career. It's something special when you have a coach of his caliber who was also a player at a very high level.

"He's not trying to make everyone emulate him or what his style was, but it worked for him and he's going to put a little of that in everyone. The way he wants you to approach the game [is] just a way of looking in the mirror at what he does because that was successful for him. It definitely worked for him, and I'll gladly be [described as] a Don Mattingly–type hitter. If you can be compared to Donnie or any great major leaguer who's been in this game, it's definitely a compliment. But to be compared to Donnie in particular—a great left-handed hitter, one I think has been overshadowed for the numbers he put up—is something special."

Casey Blake is a Dodgers veteran who has been around the block. He was impressed by Mattingly's approach as batting coach.

"First of all, as an ex-player, he has to remove his ego, if there is any at all," Blake said. "There's none of that in play. Second of all, I think he still remembers just how hard it is to hit. He certainly hasn't forgotten that. He doesn't believe that everybody ought to try to hit like him or hit like certain guys. He'll take your swing and he'll just work within it. Those are a couple of the reasons [why he is] good.

"I've heard there have been some guys over the years, some outstanding hitters, [who] tried to make [players] look and swing like them. But a good hitting coach realizes that the guy's probably been swinging like that for a reason, and he got here for a reason with that swing, so let's just work within that swing."

Even Blake, a 12-year major league veteran with more than 4,800 big-league plate appearances heading into the 2011 season, can see the benefits of Mattingly's tutelage.

"Sure," Blake said. "He's good. He knows guys' swings, he knows their routines. He knows when a guy is a little off, the things the guy is doing that are preventing him from hitting. In studying everyone's swing, he'll know something to say or point out to get [the hitter] back on the right track."

Kemp said Mattingly's résumé does in fact make a difference. He knows what "Donnie B." did as a Yankee and it carries weight—with him anyway.

"I didn't really get a chance to see him play because I was young," Kemp said. "But all you have to do is Google him or go back and look at clips or look at his numbers. He had some amazing numbers. [He was] always in the MVP running and All-Stars. He's just a great player. He is somebody you don't *have* to listen to but somebody you probably *should* listen to because he knows what he's talking about.

"[He won] Gold Gloves, so he definitely knows how to play the game and how to approach it. He tries to teach you that it's not all about just being physical. [It's also about] the mental part of the game, about going up there and not thinking too much but trying to figure out what that pitcher's going to do that day or what are his good pitches and what are his bad pitches. He always has a plan.

"He's always talking about not giving up at-bats and making pitchers work. Especially with the good pitchers, you want to make them throw as many pitches in each at-bat and try to get [them] out of there as quickly as possible.

"If [what you did] wasn't the right thing, he lets you know. And if you did [do the right thing], he lets you know, too. He's kind of quiet, but he's *not* quiet. Kind of both. It's not a look—he's a very vocal guy. In each at-bat he'll tell you what you did wrong. He has a lot of knowledge of the game."

The Dodgers hitters took a step back in 2010, even leading Mattingly to quip the batting coach might be one of the reasons Joe Torre was moving on. But it's always hard to attribute the successes or failures of a certain season to the coach in charge. The players all knew Mattingly was there for them far more than the results showed that season.

* * *

For many, including those who worked with him with the Yankees, seeing Don Mattingly in a different uniform remains a very strange thing.

"When we played against them in Los Angeles this year, it was weird for me to see him in another uniform," said Yankees coach Tony Peña.

"Posada said the same thing," Mattingly said. "It was a little different at first. Now I don't even think about it. But it was definitely a little different at first—going to Vero Beach, that first camp over there with Joe.

"But I look at it like Yogi [Berra]. He was with Houston, he was with the Mets, and you still think of Yogi with the Yankees. I think that will always be me.

"When I left, it was the right thing. I didn't leave with any animosity. I love New York, and I like the organization. I don't have any problems with anybody over there. I'm proud to have played there, and I loved the fans. I liked everything about New York and playing there. So I didn't leave with any kind of bitter taste [in my mouth]."

* * *

Preston Mattingly was the Dodgers' first draft choice in 2006, the 31st pick overall in the draft. While his dad was under-drafted because of the things people said he couldn't do (19th round by the Yankees), Mattingly's son may have been over-drafted because … well, consider the bloodline.

Regardless, Preston Mattingly, an infielder, got off to a good start, hitting .290 with a home run and 29 RBIs in rookie ball. But it went downhill from there, and the Dodgers, who had just named his dad as their manager, traded Preston to the Cleveland Indians for outfielder Roman Peña.

Minor league deals like this are made all the time, but this one involved Don Mattingly's son. "I have talked to him about it, and he is excited," Don Mattingly said after the deal was completed. "For me, I'm thankful to the organization. He had kind of fallen off in his playing time this year and really wasn't getting to play a lot. To do this for him at this time was really significant for him, and he is young enough that he still thinks he can play and he wants to go prove that."

Speaking six weeks later, Don reiterated, "I think it's the right thing. I know he's happy about it, and not [because he wanted] get away from the organization. He [didn't pan] out for them, and it was a situation where he was looking for a new start.

"[He was] looking for somebody to give him a chance and use him a little bit more. He just didn't do enough over here to move up and get

Yankees owner George Steinbrenner speaks as Mattingly formally announces his retirement in January 1997 after sitting out the 1996 season. (AP Images)

The Yankees retired Mattingly's No. 23 and dedicated his plaque in Yankee Stadium's Monument Park on August 31, 1997. (Stan Honda/AFP/Getty Images)

DONALD ARTHUR MATTINGLY
"DONNIE BASEBALL"
1982-1995

AMERICAN LEAGUE BATTING CHAMPION	1984
AMERICAN LEAGUE MVP (145 RBI)	1985
NINE-TIME GOLD GLOVE WINNER	
SIX-TIME AMERICAN LEAGUE ALL-STAR	
SET RECORD FOR MOST GRAND SLAMS IN A SEASON (6)	1987
MAJOR LEAGUE RECORD FOR MOST HOME RUNS IN	1987
SEVEN CONSECUTIVE GAMES (9) AND EIGHT	
CONSECUTIVE GAMES (10)	
10TH PLAYER IN TEAM HISTORY TO BE NAMED CAPTAIN	1991

A HUMBLE MAN OF GRACE AND DIGNITY.
A CAPTAIN WHO LED BY EXAMPLE.
PROUD OF THE PINSTRIPE TRADITION
AND DEDICATED TO THE PURSUIT OF EXCELLENCE.
A YANKEE FOREVER

DEDICATED BY
THE NEW YORK YANKEES
AUGUST 31, 1997

In 1997, Mattingly joined an elite group of Yankees including Babe Ruth, Lou Gehrig, Mickey Mantle, and Joe DiMaggio in Yankee Stadium's Monument Park. Above is Mattingly's plaque. (Jim McIsaac/Getty Images)

Mattingly Baseball Charities was formed to help inner-city baseball. Here Mattingly (left) receives tips from acclaimed groundskeeper George Toma while renovating two little league fields at Jackie Robinson Park in Harlem, N.Y., in 2005. (AP Images)

After observing young players having trouble properly holding their bats, Mattingly developed a new type of baseball bat with "V-Grip" technology. The grip takes the traditionally round handle and turns it into a triangle, moving the bat's natural resting place from the back of the hand to the knuckle joint. Mattingly shows off one of these bats in 2008. (AP Images)

After serving as a special instructor during spring training for several seasons, Mattingly (right) joined Joe Torre's staff as hitting instructor in 2004. (AP Images)

Derek Jeter and Don Mattingly, the last two Yankees team captains, discuss hitting in spring training in 2004. Jeter credits Mattingly with instilling a winning atmosphere in 1995 that led to the Yankees dynasty later that decade. (Linda Cataffo/NY Daily News Archive via Getty Images)

Yankees slugger Jason Giambi takes some tips in the batting cage from hitting coach Don Mattingly in September 2004. The Yankees set a franchise record with 242 home runs in Mattingly's first season as hitting coach. (AP Images)

Derek Jeter (right) and Mattingly (center) talk with Giants star Barry Bonds prior to a 2007 interleague game in San Francisco. (AP Images)

Joe Girardi (right) served alongside Mattingly on Joe Torre's staff in 2005 as the bench coach before leaving the Yankees to manage the Florida Marlins in 2006. When the Yankees and Torre parted ways after the 2007 season, Girardi was chosen over Mattingly to be the next Yankees manager. *(Larry W. Smith/Getty Images)*

Joe Torre (left) took over as the manager of the Los Angeles Dodgers in 2008, and Mattingly joined him as the hitting coach, wearing a major league uniform other than the Yankees' for the first time. (AP Images)

Colorado Rockies hitting coach Don Baylor (right), Mattingly's former Yankees teammate who is also sometimes referred to as "Donnie Baseball," chats with Mattingly before an August 2010 game. (AP Images)

In September 2010, Joe Torre (left) announced his retirement effective at the end of the 2010 season. Mattingly (right) was named as Torre's successor. Here the outgoing and incoming managers pose with Dodgers owner Frank McCourt. (AP Images)

Dodgers manager Don Mattingly speaks with reporters at Dodger Stadium in October 2010. (AP Images)

playing time. He wants to keep trying and that's a good thing for me.... I think the Dodgers did the right thing for him, because if you can't give him playing time—he's 22—don't hold him until he's 24 and doesn't have a chance to play anywhere, until he's too old to be playing A Ball. He's still at an age where, if he ever catches on, if they give him a chance and he catches on, he's not too old. [The Dodgers] didn't have the time. He got passed by and wasn't going to get playing time."

And it's probably not the worst thing for Preston to get out of the organization for which his father has just become the new manager. That could be something people might bring up down the road. It's petty, but it could be used against the manager.

"I'm sure it could be," Don said. "He's pretty good with it. I think he said too that he doesn't want special treatment and that type of thing. It's good all around."

Preston had batted .232 in five minor league seasons with the Dodgers. He hit just .217 with two homers and 17 RBIs with two teams (both low in the organization) in 2010, leading to the trade.

Preston is the middle of Don and Kim Mattingly's three sons and the second to play professional baseball. Eldest son Taylor was drafted by the Yankees in the 42nd round of the 2003 draft. His dad wanted him to go to college, but instead he reported to the Gulf Coast Yankees at age 18.

Taylor Mattingly, an outfielder/first baseman, went 13-for-58, all singles, in 24 games. He then suffered a shoulder injury that wiped him out for 2004 and '05. He retired from baseball and is running the Mattingly horse farm in Evansville.

"He hurt his shoulder," Don said in October 2010. "He's one of those [players who] could hit a little bit but just wasn't ready. He just didn't want to go to school."

Jordon Mattingly is the youngest of the Mattingly boys, the one who bugged George Steinbrenner for Cracker Jack on the day his dad was enshrined in Monument Park in Yankee Stadium. Don said that you could tell at a very young age that Jordon had no desire to follow in the family business.

"He was always into other things and just didn't show much interest [in baseball]," Don said. "I remember telling him, 'Don't worry about it. We'll find something you like to do.' He played some sports, but you could tell he really wasn't into it all that much."

Jordon Mattingly started college in Florida in the fall of 2010.

* * *

While they had their differences, most of the time there was never any doubt about the way George Steinbrenner felt about Don Mattingly.

"*Special.* That's the best word for [it]. A special person, special student of the game, a special everything," Steinbrenner said about Mattingly after he was done playing. "That's just the word I put on him.

"I had different guys who I term differently. I term him *special.*"

George used to call Mattingly "Jack Armstrong, All-American" and tell people that his first baseman was like a son to him.

On July 13, 2010, nine days after his 80th birthday, George M. Steinbrenner III passed away in Florida. A man Don Mattingly considered "bigger than life" was gone.

"[I remember] all the good thoughts of Mr. Steinbrenner and thoughts of the legacy that he's leaving for the organization and for what he did for the Yankees and the city of New York. [There were] some pretty big, bold statements he made over his time there with the Yankees," Mattingly shared in a telephone interview with the YES Network's Michael Kay and Jack Curry during the station's all-day tribute to the Boss, whose always-working brain brought that network to life.

"I really felt like family," Mattingly said. "He really made me feel comfortable. He'd invite me to the [Kentucky] Derby, I always recall that.... After I retired he wanted to make sure I knew he wanted me to come to spring training, wanted me to be part of it. He just always made me feel that he wanted me to be part of the family. I always felt comfortable around him."

That was the thing about Steinbrenner. Yes, it was a family, but one with a J.R. Ewing at the top. It would be an understatement to say George didn't always treat his employees well, but there were also plenty of employees who left and kept coming back. Even Mattingly had his run-ins with his boss—none bigger than between the 1988 and '89 seasons when Mattingly, tired of the things Steinbrenner had said about him in the media, confronted George on the phone.

Steinbrenner's comments describing how highly he regarded his star first baseman were played for Mattingly on the air the day Steinbrenner died.

"It makes me feel good," Mattingly said. "Obviously, I don't take too much [from] what people say and things like that, but coming from him … you want to earn the respect of people [for whom] you work. You want to feel like you did a good job for them and they appreciated what you did. For him to say those things makes me feel good about my time there, and I've always felt that way.

"That's the funny thing—I loved New York, and I love coming back. I loved playing there. I feel like it's my home. And [Steinbrenner] just made you feel like family. So in a sense you feel like you're one of his boys. It's just a good feeling."

Thinking back, Mattingly said, "He wanted to fight for perfection, to be the best and to keep striving for it. And he would do anything he could to try to bring that out in you. When you fought back and fought for yourself, he had respect for that, too. It shows both sides, [that he was] demanding but also [that he had a] human side, that he understood what you were talking about as a person."

That's what happened in the conversation between the two during the off-season between 1988 and '89. Dallas Green asked Mattingly to call Steinbrenner, Mattingly said he would, and he did. He had his say and George hung up the phone, wishing him "good luck." Mattingly was sure he was gone, sure he would be traded, but it never happened. The pair remained close after that.

When asked if there was one story he would tell his kids about Steinbrenner, Mattingly said, "There are so many things he did. I could tell them so many, like him bringing me over to Louisville for the Derby. He wanted me to be part of it when his horse was going to run in the Derby. We went to the paddock [together]. It made me feel so good that he wanted me to be part of that. [There are] all kinds of stories like that."

There are two events in Mattingly's career that may well have gone differently had George had more to do with them.

The first was when manager Stump Merrill ordered Mattingly to cut his hair or be benched. Mattingly didn't, and he did in fact sit. When asked if that would have happened had George not been suspended from baseball at that time, Mattingly said, "I'm sure he wouldn't have liked [the hair], but he would have handled it differently.

"I don't think he was behind it. I have a pretty good idea who it was, though it doesn't really matter. It's not a big issue at all. It's a funny thing that happened in the past. If [Steinbrenner] was in charge of the organization… it would have been handled a lot differently."

The other event, much more important, took place when the Yankees were looking for a manager for the 2008 season. Mattingly, the longtime favorite of the owner, interviewed for the job. Steinbrenner, suffering the effects of his declining health, was present for the interview but he wasn't really *there.*

"During my interview, he was in the room but he wasn't," Mattingly said a month or so before Steinbrenner's death. "If he was *in* the room, he would have run the show—and he wasn't running the show. It was sad for me…because he was in the room but obviously not himself. He just let everybody else run the meeting. I know Mr. Steinbrenner well enough to know if he had all his wits about him at that point, he'd have been running the show right there. So it was a little sad."

Mike Kay more than hinted and Jack Curry agreed that a hale and healthy Steinbrenner would have wanted Don Mattingly as the next manager of the New York Yankees.

"He recruited him personally to be the batting coach," Kay said. "By bringing him into the dugout as one of Joe Torre's lieutenants, I think that was the first step to prepare him to be the Yankees manager. It was always George's dream because of [Mattingly's] star quality and the fact that he respected Mattingly so much."

Said Curry, "Looking at Don Mattingly and the legend he had been as a Yankee, from an MVP and everything that goes with that, I think there's a good chance you're right [about Steinbrenner wanting Mattingly as the next manager]."

That interview was the last time Mattingly talked to Steinbrenner.

"The one thing about playing in New York, playing for him, is you can complain about [how] he gets on you and he's tough and all that, [but] who cares as a player, really?" Mattingly said. "One thing you knew when you went to spring training with the Yankees was you didn't really come there just to play .500. You didn't come there to get a little better, [either]. You wanted to win it all—and that was the best thing about playing in New York. You'd be in some other cities—they'd play .500, and they were happy. That just wasn't the case with us—and I thought that was great. I loved that part of it."

Broadcaster Suzyn Waldman remembers a story from Mattingly's playing days while Steinbrenner was suspended.

"We were in Anaheim and had just an awful, awful road trip," she said. "All of a sudden, everyone was talking about the road trip and the perception the team was dead in the water. I remember Donnie saying something like, 'You know that's the difference without George here. Sometimes George did the wrong things, but you know he always cared.'

"It came right out of his mouth and it made me stop and think because everybody obviously had fights with George. The perception was that he was meddling, but not to Donnie. He knew immediately that something was wrong because [Steinbrenner] wasn't there, because at least he cared."

Both men wanted to win every game the Yankees played. "I think it's part Mr. Steinbrenner, I think it's part New York, I think it's part the

Don Mattingly's Official Statement on the Passing of George Steinbrenner:

"I am deeply saddened to hear the news of George Steinbrenner's passing. His vision, passion, and commitment to winning recharged the New York Yankees and revolutionized the game. I remember a man driven to succeed. He was the owner, 'the Boss,' and No. 1 fan of the Yankees. Our relationship was built on mutual respect. I will never forget and always be grateful for how he treated me and my family both during my playing days and after I retired. I will miss him very much and extend my deepest condolences to his wife, Joan, and all the members of the Steinbrenner family."

—*Dodgers Hitting Coach Don Mattingly*

importance that he put on winning and the type of people he brought in…. And it's because of fans of New York, to be honest with you, too, because they demand it," Mattingly said.

"It's such a great place to play because it's *so* demanding, because every day is a new day and we needed to win the game. That kind of mentality is, to me, the perfect baseball mentality. It pushes guys to be better, it forces them to concentrate on a daily basis. It doesn't allow you to rest on your laurels or get caught up in what you did in the past. I think it's the perfect atmosphere, and he was definitely part of that."

* * *

Mattingly was thrilled to have the chance to come home to the new Yankee Stadium for the unveiling of the George Steinbrenner monument in Monument Park in center field. He and Joe Torre flew cross-country for the event, which took place on a Dodgers off-day.

Even though Mattingly insists there were no hard feelings over his leaving the Yankees with Torre—after he wasn't chosen as the manager's replacement—there still seemed to be a bit of a chasm between the club and one of its all-time greats, as was the case with Torre.

But in late September 2010, just days after Mattingly was officially named to replace Torre as the Dodgers manager for 2011, the Yankees unveiled their new monument of Steinbrenner in center field at the Yankee Stadium. Both Mattingly—who meant so much to the organization as a player and coach but hadn't been back to Yankee Stadium since leaving after the 2007 season—and Torre—who managed the team to world championships No. 23 through 26—were there.

Yankees captain Derek Jeter said, "It's great that they get the opportunity to come back to the Stadium. I'm sure they'll be well-received by everyone."

That night, Mattingly said, "I have no bridges to burn. I love the Yankees. They've been part of me [throughout] my whole life. They helped me grow up and taught me about playing this game. I love coming back to New York, no question about it…. I walked out thinking I'd always come back."

Both Mattingly and Torre were part of the procession that made its way around the warning track out to center field.

Looking back six weeks later, Mattingly said, "I was really comfortable. I was happy [because I wanted] to see the stadium. I've always wanted to go back [to Yankee Stadium] when we were in [New York] to play the Mets in the last couple of years. Last year I think we had a rainout and we had a split double-header or regular double-header, so it just didn't work out. And the year before I wanted to go, too, and something else happened.

"So I'd been wanting to go back to the stadium. I haven't been avoiding it—I've been trying to go back. So to get a chance to go back and be part of the ceremony for Mr. Steinbrenner was a good feeling. It really was. I was really happy on that day. I looked at it a lot like Yogi coming back. Yogi was gone so long and then George…something happened with [Berra's] museum or whatever, but Yogi went back. I really felt like Joe needed to go back, [too]. I felt really good about that. From deep down in my Yankees roots, it made me feel good that the Yankees had him back. It was a good feeling.

"Mr. Steinbrenner did so much for me. He did stuff people don't know about. He flew me in to get my back surgery. He flew his plane to Indiana, picked me up, brought me there, took care of me the whole time I was there. He had me in a hotel, and he wouldn't have let me even think about paying for anything. He did so many different things."

It was on that night that Mattingly revealed that general manager Brian Cashman had called him and offered him a job with the club—after the Yanks had hired Joe Girardi to replace Torre.

"Cash had called me and said that he picked Joe and he wanted me to kind of stay on," Mattingly said. "At that point, there was no bitterness at all for me.

"[I] didn't think it was the right thing to come back at that time. That was the reason I didn't take it. I didn't really want Joe [Girardi] to have to deal with that every time the team struggled for five days. I didn't think it was fair to him. And I think it was time for me to just move forward."

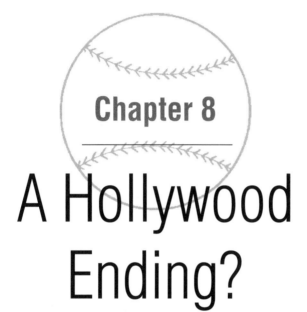

Chapter 8

A Hollywood Ending?

"I think his humility is going to help a lot. He's not approaching it from the vantage point that he's going to be perfect and not going to make mistakes. He's realistic that you do make mistakes but you learn from them, and that's how you become a winner."

—Frank McCourt, Dodgers Owner

"He didn't know the rule. If he is the next manager, the guy he's replacing didn't know it either, so that's the way it goes."

—Joe Torre on Don Mattingly's pitching-change
mistake against the Giants in July 2010.

The Dodgers and Giants, rival franchises from New York who moved west together in 1958, were throwing at each other in 2010. Torre and bench coach Bob Schaefer were both tossed, leaving batting coach Don Mattingly in charge for the rest of the game.

Flash forward to the top of the ninth inning. The Dodgers led 5–4, and the Giants had runners on second and third with one out when Mattingly had Jonathan Broxton intentionally walk Aubrey Huff to load the bases and bring up Andres Torres.

Mattingly came out to the mound for a conference that was attended by his infielders. As he turned to leave, he had barely stepped off the mound surface when first baseman James Loney called out a question on positioning. Mattingly turned, and with umpire Adrian Johnson yelling for him not to go back onto the mound, turned back to talk to the player.

Out came Giants manager Bruce Bochy, who once nailed then-Dodgers manager Grady Little for the same thing, and he told the umpires a change [in pitchers] had to be made. Broxton was then ordered off the mound, and George Sherrill—who had just been placed on outright waivers, cleared them, and returned—was summoned. He was supposed to get as long as he needed to warm up, but Johnson cut him off at eight pitches. It turned out to be the second mistake the umpires made in the situation.

Sherrill, not ready, gave up a two-run double to Torres, and the game was lost. It was one of many losses suffered by the Dodgers in the second half of the season after having been as much as 12 games better than .500 in June.

At least one Dodgers insider said later that the way Broxton had been pitching, it wouldn't have mattered if he stayed out there—but that was another story. The story that got the attention was Mattingly's miscue.

"I didn't realize I was off the dirt, number one," Mattingly said. "You don't realize that you're off, you're just turning around and talking. Afterward I read that rule and even if I would have been off the dirt, on the grass, and talked to Loney and he would have talked to the pitcher, then that would have counted as a trip. I couldn't walk off the dirt.... Loney asked me a question, I told him something and kept walking. I never get back on the dirt. If he talked to the pitcher at that point, they could technically say it [was a trip].... If he walked over to the pitcher, or if I told him something and he was over by first and the pitcher walked over to talk to him, it could technically be called a trip."

Mattingly said he heard Johnson's calls. "[I heard him] just as I turned around...I had gotten my second foot barely off...because I turned to talk to Loney," he said. "I hear as I'm walking, 'Don't go up there, don't go up there,' and I'm already up there. As soon as I turned I was basically up there."

But here's the thing: the umpires were more at fault than Mattingly. Putting it simply, a manager can't make two trips to the mound with the same batter at the plate. The rule was put in place to prevent stalling, which allows for a reliever to get more throws in the bullpen. The rule, 8.06 in the Official Baseball Rules, is specific:

> *In a case where a manager has made his first trip to the mound and then returns the second time to the mound in the same inning with the same pitcher in the game and the same batter at bat, after being warned by the umpire that he cannot return to the mound, the manager shall be removed from the game and the pitcher required to pitch to the batter until he is retired or gets on base. After the batter is retired, or becomes a base runner, then this pitcher must be removed from the game. The manager should be notified that his pitcher will be removed from the game after he pitches to one hitter, so he can have a substitute pitcher warmed up. The substitute pitcher will be allowed eight preparatory pitches or more if in the umpire's judgment circumstances justify.*

According to the rules, Mattingly should have been the third Dodgers manager ejected from the game, Broxton should have faced Torres while Sherrill warmed up in the bullpen, and Broxton should then have left after facing Torres. Things could have turned out differently.

When Major League Baseball sent word to the coast that the umpires were in the wrong, the reaction of crew chief Tim McClelland was rather typical of the problems the game has had with its umpires these days.

"I am not of the opinion [that's the way the rule should have been applied]," McClelland said. "The league is of that opinion. It's a difference of opinion in a situation that's not covered.

"[With] a defiant manager, in that situation, the pitcher has to pitch. We were processing what had happened [before Bochy came out]. I have never seen that situation in my 28 years as an umpire, and I've heard about it only once. [Whether he was defiant] was part of our discussion."

Summing up how he felt after it happened, Mattingly said, "Obviously we're not playing [well], and it cost us a chance to win the game. With Brox in the game, the bases were loaded there, but we felt like we could get out of that. So [I'm not feeling] good."

"I wasn't mad at the umpires so much," he said later. "I was mad at myself more than anything. Even though they got it wrong, I was still wrong. [Yankees trainer] Steve Donahue called me and said, 'Bochy shouldn't have done that.' I said, 'It's Bochy's job to do that. That's exactly what he's supposed to do.'"

"It was a mistake," Torre said, noting that he was told by MLB vice president Bob Watson that the umpires erred twice. "Broxton should have been allowed to pitch to the hitter and Donnie should have been thrown out, according to the rules. I was consumed with the Sherrill thing. McClelland told Donnie he'd have as many pitches as he needed. The umpire behind the plate stopped him at eight. McClelland said, 'Ready?' and George said, 'I guess so,' and that was that."

The Dodgers didn't protest.

"It's our [responsibility] to make the protest," Torre said. "The people [who were] supposed to do it weren't even in the dugout. That's me. It was just a screw-up all the way around. We had the right to protest, and we didn't do that. The umpire sort of messed up, too."

It all led to a rough night for Mattingly. "Sleeping wasn't so tough. Getting to sleep was a lot tougher," Mattingly said. "It took me a while to get to sleep, I'll say that."

Mattingly had also made a mistake with a spring training lineup card in Taiwan, apparently failing to read the card filled out by bench coach Bob Schaefer and presenting a different one at home plate, which led the Dodgers to bat out of order.

But with Torre and Schaefer suspended, Mattingly held the reins against the Giants again the next night. The Dodgers won 2–0 behind Chad Billingsley's shutout. No trips to the mound were required.

"It was awesome, especially after [the previous] night. I know he felt bad about what happened. You just feel terrible for the guy because you know how bad he feels," said veteran Casey Blake, who homered in the game. "I love that guy. Just like Joe, you want to play hard for him. It's nice to get that [first win] under his belt."

Torre had a little fun with it. "I told Donnie [before the game] he was managing tonight," he said. "He said, 'You sure?'"

"Seriously," Torre said. "That has nothing to do with his managerial ability. It's a reaction thing. He turned around to talk to the player. It's something you learn, and you move on. It could happen to me at some point."

In the aftermath, Mattingly said the incident did nothing to kill his desire to manage, something he will do in 2011.

"Great players come up, and you know they're going to make mistakes when they get here," he told Dodgers.com. "It doesn't mean they can't play, and I look at [managing] the same way. It doesn't change my thinking that I'm going to be a good manager someday. [It was] part of a painful process right here for me. It's not enjoyable."

Mattingly harkened back to his early playing days.

"My first game in New York was Yankee Stadium on Opening Day," he said. "I got like three plays that were all crazy. [But] you suck it up. The place is booing you, but that's just part of it. You just suck it up, and at the end you answer the questions—and you know you don't make those mistakes again. The way I look at it is that it's not the first mistake I've made, and it's not going to be the last. But…it's the last time I make *that* mistake."

Torre dared critics to bury Mattingly. "If that's what you're going to judge him on," he said. "There's a whole lot more to him than [him] making a foot fault out there. He's certainly not shy about taking responsibility… and that's part of why I felt he was going to be a good coach and why he'll be a good manager."

The departing Dodgers manager also said, "I know one thing—the guy that got him was the same guy who almost got me. I stopped myself… It was James Loney. Donnie went out and told James what to do, and as he left James wanted to be reassured what he was doing and Donnie went back. He did that to me—I think we were in San Diego—and I went back and

I turned around and [turned back around and] kept walking. But Donnie walked back.

"Donnie didn't know he was off the dirt because he just barely was. He had one foot in the air. If he had brought that foot down on the dirt without putting it in the grass, I bet it would have been okay."

* * *

On September 17, 2010, Don Mattingly was officially named the 2011 manager of the Los Angeles Dodgers. It became clear that the deal had been worked out even before the season began.

"I turned down an opportunity to talk with Washington, and I talked with Cleveland. I had a meeting with [Dodgers owner Frank] McCourt and [general manager] Ned [Colletti]," Mattingly said. "They knew there were going to be [other teams] wanting to talk to me. But the feeling I got from those conversations made me feel good enough to know they were interested in me, and that was all I needed to hear."

When Joe Torre was hired to manage the club for the 2008 season, Colletti told Torre that in the interest of establishing continuity in the organization, he would like for Torre's coaching staff to include a person who would be a logical heir apparent.

"I told Joe I would like to have a successor on the staff," Colletti said. "He said there were a couple of guys he would like to bring with him, and that one of them was Don Mattingly—not only as a coach but as somebody who could one day succeed him.

"We wanted continuity here. We wanted somebody who understood our players and understood our organization."

Said Torre, "I felt this ballclub needed a different voice. A younger voice." Mattingly might have been the heir apparent even then, but he didn't even start the 2008 season with the Dodgers. Family problems forced him to be away from the team for the first half of the season, so Mike Easler stepped in as the hitting coach. Mattingly returned after the All-Star break and worked for 2½ seasons as Torre's batting coach, also taking notes on what a manager should and should not do.

Then came the hiring, a formality to those on the inside but a shock to people around the country who said there was no way Mattingly would ever get this job—people who predicted that Triple A manager Tim Wallach or someone else would become the Dodgers' fourth manager in six years.

"I know one thing: I have to be myself," Mattingly said the day he was officially hired. "There will be parts of Joe in me, parts of Billy Martin in me, parts of Lou Piniella in me, and parts of Dallas Green in me. All the guys I played for and played against, they all affected the way I think the game should be played. If I'm going to do something, I'm going to go for it. I have to go with my beliefs. It may be a different generation, but there is only one way to play the game, and that is the right way.

"I know people are going to question it, and that's understandable, but in my heart, I know I can do this. There's a feeling inside of me that says I'm ready."

Brooklyn/Los Angeles Dodgers Managers Since the Start of the 1950 Season:

Burt Shotton—1950
Charlie Dressen—1951–1953
Walter Alston—1954–1976
Tommy Lasorda—1976–1996
Bill Russell—1996–1998
Glenn Hoffman—1998
Davey Johnson—1999–2000
Jim Tracy—2001–2005
Grady Little—2006–2007
Joe Torre—2008–2010
Don Mattingly—2011–?

Said Colletti, "If you watch Donnie interact with people and watch his work ethic, and you didn't know who it was and then someone told you it was Don Mattingly, you'd be shocked that someone with his background and accomplishments had that kind of work ethic."

Added McCourt, "I think his humility is going to help a lot. He's not approaching it from the vantage point that he's going to be perfect and not going to make mistakes. He's realistic that you do make mistakes but you learn from them, and that's how you become a winner."

* * *

When asked about emotional right fielder Andre Ethier after getting officially hired as the Dodgers' new manager, Mattingly told ESPN, "You just have to make sure he doesn't disconnect. Sometimes he gets so mad, he'll disconnect and start throwing at-bats away. That's just his personality, that's the way he plays, and that's fine. But you can't let him get so mad that he disconnects and starts throwing at-bats away.

"He's changed his approach a hair—just a little bit to be more aggressive, more willing to pull balls. He used to only want to take balls to left field, and he has power that way. But at Dodger Stadium, we always talk about keeping the ball out of the air to left field. If you're going to hit the ball that way, it needs to be down the line, it needs to be something sharp because there are so many outs made over there. For every ball you hit out of the park at Dodger Stadium to left field, you're going to fly out 20 times. You can't really be lofting balls that way at Dodger Stadium. It's a big field and we play a lot of night games [in which] the ball just isn't going to jump. When it's cool at night, it's not going to carry. If we played a ton of day games, it'd be a different story."

* * *

Here's something you might not know about Midwesterner Don Mattingly as he takes over as manager of the Dodgers: "The first time I came to

California [as a player], I loved it," he said. "The weather, the cool nights, the laid-back [vibe] away from the field. I like that a lot. This place fits my personality really well. I live at the beach. I like it a lot, and I chill away from the field. It allows me to be somebody different."

Mattingly loved New York, too—everything about it. So much for not being able to take the farm boy away from the farm.

* * *

To say Mattingly wasn't welcomed with open arms by the Los Angeles media would be an understatement. Many labeled him a failure long before his first game as the new Dodgers skipper.

In the *Los Angeles Times*, Bill Plaschke's first column on the change was printed as follows:

Frank McCourt stepped to the dais, stared down at Don Mattingly, and began another new Dodgers era with a question.

"Are you ready?"

I would propose perhaps a more appropriate question.

Are you kidding?

The announcement Friday that Joe Torre would be quitting as Dodgers manager at the end of this season was sweet and sentimental for the five seconds it took to add that Mattingly would be his successor, at which point it was just scary.

How does a dugout that once was run by the likes of Walter Alston and Tom Lasorda open its top step to a guy with no previous managerial experience at any level? And why do the Dodgers do this without at least interviewing somebody else, anybody else, not even a minority even though baseball approved the hiring process.

"I feel like I've been working for this for a long time," said Mattingly, 49, who has seven years of major league coaching experience. "I'm ready."

Here's guessing most Dodgers fans aren't quite ready for him.

Plaschke wasn't alone.

One fan said, "The times that Don Mattingly has been acting manager, he's made some decisions that Coach Buttermaker of the Bad News Bears wouldn't have made."

"Do you really want a manager-in-training? Wouldn't you want to bring in somebody who can stabilize the team with all this going on?" said another.

Some felt as if the Dodgers had gone out on Sepulveda Boulevard and chosen the first guy off the street to come and run the club.

They didn't. Instead, they took one of the best players of his era, a guy who has studied the game from top to bottom since he was a kid. It was *Don Bleeping Mattingly*!

"It's baseball, and I've been around the game a long time," Mattingly said. "In my heart, I know I can do this. [I have] belief in myself that I can do anything I put my mind to."

Will it work? Who knows? Joe Torre's arrival in New York was greeted with a "Clueless Joe" headline. (The headline referred to Torre's cluelessness in what he was getting himself into with George Steinbrenner, but that's not how some took it.) The Phillies were ripped for hiring Charlie Manuel, and how did that work out for them? The list of panned managerial hirings and people then proven wrong is endless.

The fact is, you just don't know. All a team can do is take a guess and see what happens.

Mattingly has inarguably stepped into a tough situation. The divorcing McCourts have been fighting for the team, which went from 12 games better than .500 in June to finish 80–82 amid a rash of injuries. The club was losing money. There was little indication there was enough budget to get Mattingly the players he would need. And, let's face it, no manager wins without players.

On top of all that, the Dodgers were in a division that not only featured brilliant pitching staffs in both San Francisco and San Diego, but stud right-hander Ubaldo Jimenez pitching for a pretty good Colorado Rockies team in Denver.

Going into 2011 with an untested manager appeared to be the least of the club's problems.

Then again, the Dodgers made it almost all the way to the World Series in 2008 and 2009, and many of those same players will be there when Mattingly begins his managerial career.

And at least Mattingly won't have Manny Ramirez to put up with.

"Over the past three years, I've had the opportunity to work with Don closely and have gotten to know him both personally and professionally, and I'm convinced that he's the right person to lead the Dodgers," general manager Ned Colletti said in a release that day. "His work ethic is unparalleled, his baseball knowledge is vast, and his leadership skills have been established during more than three decades in professional baseball.

"Donnie has also learned alongside the best in the business. Joe Torre has been a great friend, a strong leader and an incredible presence for this organization, and I cannot thank him enough for his service to the Dodgers. I respect his decision to step aside and I look forward to the day [when] I can watch him take his rightful place in Cooperstown among baseball's legends."

Mattingly worked for Torre. He played for the likes of Billy Martin, Lou Piniella, and Buck Showalter. Now he would be getting *his* chance. He got it amid controversy surrounding the Dodgers. Many wanted Triple A manager Tim Wallach to get the job in L.A.. Others, like reporter Bill Madden in New York, wrote that there was no chance Mattingly would get the job. Columnist Peter Gammons said it looked like Mattingly would be left out in the cold.

Then came the news.

Bang.

Just like that.

"The opportunity to manage the Los Angeles Dodgers is truly an honor," Mattingly said that day. "There are few organizations in the world with the history, tradition, and track record of success as the Dodgers. I'm looking forward to continuing what I came here to accomplish with Joe, and that's to win a world championship."

Speaking two days after the end of the regular season, and having just finished a second straight day of meetings, Mattingly was excited and ready to go to the Arizona Fall League to get a 32-game taste of managing.

"In confirming Mattingly's ascension to manager after the season, Colletti cited Mattingly's work ethic and leadership and there is no denying either," Bill Madden wrote in the *New York Daily News*. "So tireless was Mattingly's work with the Dodgers hitters he was virtually invisible to the media, while as captain of the Yankees his clubhouse leadership was the one attribute of all others that prompted Steinbrenner to prematurely anoint him as a future Yankees manager. But as Lou Piniella [who also never had managed anywhere when Steinbrenner tapped him to replace Billy Martin as Yankees skipper in 1986] can tell him, 'There's a lot more to managing than hard work and being perceived as a leader.' Or as Connie Mack so famously said, 'Pitching is 90 percent of baseball,' and, until proven otherwise, there are serious questions about Mattingly's ability to manage a pitching staff, especially since he's never had to do it. Indeed, it is suspected Mattingly's relationship with the core Dodgers hitters, James Loney, Andre Ethier, Matt Kemp, was what most prompted Colletti to give him the job."

Mattingly supporters, who seemed to include anyone who has ever known the guy, were behind him 100 percent.

One of them, Showalter, who had only recently taken over in Baltimore, bristled when asked about Mattingly never having done this before.

"He's done it before. He's done it every night of his life," Showalter said as he dressed for a game at Fenway Park soon after Mattingly got the job. "We used to sit around and talk about it all the time, because he wanted to learn. He'd say, 'Why? What are you thinking there? Got it.' He'd stick his head in [my office] and say, 'Walk me through that last night.'

"He's done it every night of his life—and I think because of who Donnie was, the type of player he was, he didn't run particularly well, a lot of people said he couldn't hit for power, a lot of people said he was going to be just an okay fielder—he always, not overachieved, but wanted to prove people wrong.

"He's going to have that sympathy for a guy who says, 'Why am I sitting against left-handers?' because they told Donnie that at 19, 'Well, you're not going to play against left-handers.' Why? He wasn't a great runner, great thrower, or a huge power-early guy—but he's done everything.... I don't think he's going to turn his back on any possibility with a player. He's not going to let anybody pigeonhole a guy and say 'he's this, he's that, he's whatever.'

"Donnie will be blunt. You're not going to have to worry about what he's thinking because he's going to be honest to a fault. You may not always like what he's going to tell you, but you're going to know it's true from his heart—it's not something that comes because he doesn't like you. Donnie will like everybody, [I'll] tell you that. He *wants* to like you. And he likes baseball players, which a lot of people miss."

The people in L.A. clearly weren't convinced.

Wrote Plaschke:

> "Mattingly, a former New York Yankees first baseman, was a brilliant hitter who spent the game on a corner, a quiet sort with a thoughtful demeanor who doesn't have bush-league bench experience or the credibility of championship rings—14 years as a Yankee and not one World Series appearance—to give him the necessary juice.
>
> Usually, General Manager Ned Colletti plays it smart, but this time he clearly played it safe, and for a weary organization that needs more energy and edge, it just doesn't make sense."

A quiet sort? Interesting, considering what Showalter said about No. 23's leadership with the Yankees. "The players wanted to please Donnie," he said, and that was back when Mattingly was a player.

And while it's true these Dodgers kids may not know all that much about Don Mattingly the player, they have gotten to know Don Mattingly the man, the guy who works hard and expects others to work as hard as he does.

Showalter remembered the story of how Ruben Sierra circled the bases in an inappropriate manner after his first home run as a Yankee, making that wide swoop out of the batter's box before continuing.

Mattingly took control.

"There were so many things like that where Don said, 'I got it, I got it.'" Showalter said. "Well, guess what—*he's* now got it. He better be looking for somebody like him in his clubhouse. And good luck, because there ain't any. There aren't a lot of those guys."

Showalter said the players will know soon enough who's leading them.

"It's like I tell guys, 'You have about a two-week window. They really don't care what your career was and what you did [before],'" he said. "[He's] going to have some guys who don't even know who he is. But Donnie has so much substance, it'll play out. And the great thing with Donnie is that he has no agenda. He has a pure heart…he doesn't have an ego. He's just going to try and do what's right and that usually works.

"I think [his players] know that he has a pure heart. There's no phoniness to him. One thing you can sniff out, because we play 200 games counting spring training, seven days a week…if you got a strength it'll show up, if you got a weakness it'll show up. And phonies…get sniffed out really fast.… Donnie has none of that."

"The thing about Donnie is he's still the same guy he was then," said Bob Schaefer, who managed Mattingly in A Ball. "He hasn't changed. He never got a big head. He never [projected], 'I'm Don Mattingly, who are you?' I always say, 'I coached him before he was Don Mattingly'—but he's still Don Mattingly to me. I followed him throughout his career and even coached against him for four or five years when I was in Kansas City. He's as good a guy as there is, and I think he'll be a really good manager."

Showalter cited Mattingly's decision to retire when he did—amid back woes and the need to be at home with his sons—as an example of how pure of heart his former minor-league teammate really is.

"Some people talk about it. Some people do it," Showalter said. "Mattingly just said, 'That's it—I need to be home with my family and my back's not good enough.... That's the most important thing: the impact I have on the people I brought into the world.' A lot of people would ask, 'What's the real story?' Well, that *is* the real story with him. It is.

"He'll have some problems with people who are putting themselves above the team, I can tell you that.

"I'm glad he's getting an opportunity. He's done it the right way. There's no job beneath him."

When the 2010 season started, there was a general feeling that it would be Mattingly who would succeed Torre—who would turn 70 during the season—when he ultimately stepped down. Mattingly interviewed in New York and had a phone chat with the Cleveland folks, but he turned down a chance to interview in Washington. He said that he backed off because Colletti wanted him to be patient for the obvious reasons.

Late in the season, though, Gammons reported that it was owner Frank McCourt who denied Mattingly permission to talk to the Indians. As a coach, Mattingly's contract ran through December 31. That date was too late for the Indians, who hired Manny Acta on October 25.

Mattingly, speaking in June 2010 said, "[Indians general manager] Mark [Shapiro] needed a really quick decision—a decision I couldn't give him as quickly as he wanted. I'm not saying [the Cleveland job] was my job or anything like that, but he wanted to know what I thought was going to happen with the Dodgers. Obviously, at that point, I didn't know that either, but they'd shown an interest to me at a level that told me that they wanted me around here. I relayed that to [Shapiro], and he had to make a decision from there. I don't know all his parts but he had a timetable too...."

He had to make a decision, and he wanted to make it sooner rather than later. I really couldn't have given him a decision that quickly."

If Gammons was right, there was no chance that was going to happen. But then came word it was a done deal. Chaos? Just everyday life for the Dodgers.

Chaotic was the way things went for McCourt and the Dodgers in 2010. The owner was involved in a bitter divorce proceeding with his wife, the future of the once-proud franchise was up for grabs, and the team lost, failing to make the playoffs.

* * *

The game has changed. Consider Don Mattingly's take on one of the changes:

"Think about it," he said. "In games in the past [when] you had a six-run lead in the ninth and the pitcher came in and threw a bunch of breaking balls, guys would be yelling out of the dugout, 'Challenge somebody.' When you had the big lead in the old days the feeling was, *Okay, let's go, I'm not going to come up here trying to trick you.* It's totally different now. It can be a seven- or eight-run game, and guys [will throw] a split first pitch."

* * *

With just weeks to go in the season, Torre's departure was considered a *fait accompli*, but Mattingly was anything but a sure bet to become the next manager. The Wallach speculation was strong. But not getting the job would have been a bitter pill for Mattingly to swallow—especially after not being able to further pursue the Cleveland opportunity.

Mattingly was getting ready to manage the Phoenix Desert Dogs in the Arizona Fall League, a team slated to have several Dodgers prospects. The short season there would comprise his first extended managerial experience.

Weeks earlier in Philadelphia, Torre said, "[Mattingly's] going to make some mistakes, and he's going to have some growing pains…we all make mistakes. I think the trick about making mistakes is learning from them, not dwelling on them.

"There's a lot to Donnie, and he's certainly not lazy, as far as the mental part of this thing, either."

Others, speaking before Mattingly officially got the job, predicted managerial success.

"I definitely see that in the future," said Phillies' manager Charlie Manuel. "He's a baseball guy. He loves the game, and he's had a lot of success in it. He definitely has the qualifications, and I think he'd be good at it.

"He's been around the right people…he's been fortunate in some ways, but he's also set himself around the right kind of people and that's good."

When Mattingly got the job, Brian Cashman, the general manager who didn't hire him in New York, said, "I think it's great. I'm happy for him. I sent him a text the other day when I heard it. It's fabulous.

"I know how hard Donnie has worked for this. He's done it the right way. He hasn't politicked for anything. He's been a sponge. He's wanted to learn from the best. He's been with Joe Torre for forever it seems like now. He's a great baseball man and he was a worthy candidate."

Asked by Mike Francesa on WFAN in New York that day if Mattingly would succeed as a manager, Cashman said, "I think he will. And I think being in a position to manage some games—he's going to go to the Arizona Fall League—[will] help him.

"He's going to be fine. He's got a great demeanor, and he's a knowledge-able guy. He's not going to panic or overreact. He has a lot of huge attributes. If you give him some quality talent then he'll run with it, there's no doubt about it."

But like everyone else, Cashman just couldn't *know* what to expect.

"The only drawback is that he's never managed in the minor leagues, and that's big," said Larry Bowa, who coached third base for the Dodgers under Torre. "[As a coach], you're sitting on the bench, and somebody says, 'What do you think here?' And you say, 'Well. …' Now, as a manager, it's boom, boom, boom, boom. But I think that because of his knowledge he'll be able to do it. He might have some problems early [on], but I think he's going to make adjustments."

Jeff Schulz, Mattingly's high school teammate who had a cup of coffee in the big leagues, predicted success. "He's been under Torre for seven years [in New York and Los Angeles]," Schulz told the *Evansville Courier*. "What Don has going for him is that he's old-school … he loves the game. He's the guy who will stay up late [watching video]. When he puts the uniform on, it's do or die. … Part of his happiness is being on the ballfield. He always reached the top. He was one of the better players, and his next step is to be a manager."

Added Quentin Merkel, Mattingly's high school coach and an admirer since Mattingly was a young kid, "I feel he will do an excellent job. Don is very dedicated and hardworking. Don has gotten himself ready for this opportunity by being a hitting coach and a bench coach."

Mattingly was excited about getting needed experience in the Arizona Fall League.

"I'm looking forward to that. Just mechanically, doing it," he said. "The baseball part you don't worry about so much. But mechanically, having to make the decisions. … You sit here and watch games and [think], *You have to bring this guy in or do this, or play the infield in or we're going to play the line, or we're playing for two or we're playing halfway*. As the game goes on, you sit there and think the whole time. But it's still different from mechanically making that decision."

"Just actually walking out to the mound … you can't take a step off, you have to make sure you say everything you want to say, that everybody's clear, before you walk away. That's just mechanically doing it—it's not the baseball that got screwed up that night [when he made a mistake on the mound in the ninth inning of a game]. It's the mechanically doing it. That's the part … I'm glad I'm getting the opportunity to do that."

Infielder Jamey Carroll, who was excited to have the chance to play for Mattingly in 2011, heard all the negative talk and said, "I've heard the mixed emotions from a lot of fans about [Mattingly] being a manager. But at the same time, he has proved that he deserves the opportunity."

Not all the media reaction was negative. Mike Waldner of the *Long Beach Press-Telegram* made comparisons to former Dodgers manager and great Walter Alston and didn't understand the backlash on the Mattingly thing. He wrote:

> Torre endorsed Mattingly without hesitation. Think about this for a moment. The same people who hold Torre in high esteem are quick to disregard his opinion on what it takes to manage the Dodgers.
>
> Torre was given his first job as a manager without previous experience. The Dodgers, anticipating protests, provided a list of others in the same boat, such as Dusty Baker, Bud Black, Lou Piniella, and Ozzie Guillen.
>
> Not only had Torre not managed, he had not been a coach at any level before he made out his first lineup card.
>
> Mattingly has those seven years' service as a coach, six as hitting coach for the Yankees and Dodgers, plus one in New York as Torre's bench coach.
>
> Beyond this, and despite the fact that Bob Schaefer is the current Dodgers bench coach, Torre said he has consulted Mattingly regularly on in-game decisions for the past couple of seasons.
>
> McCourt/Colletti could have/should have gone after Baker, currently managing in Cincinnati, because his contract is over following this season.
>
> This said, the key to the near future is not the manager. It is the ability of management, no matter who ends up owning the team, to reverse the downward trend of the second half of this season. The holes on the roster are large and looking as if they are about to become larger.

This prompted one observer at the goodbye-Joe-hello-Don press conference to shake his head and, rather than applaud, say, "Poor Don."

* * *

Don Mattingly knows there are those out there who weren't exactly 100 percent behind the Dodgers hiring him to be their next manager. Being honest, some treated it as a joke perpetrated on the fans in the middle of the McCourt divorce case and all that's gone with it. Others forgot—or just don't know—who he is.

Mattingly takes it all like he's taken everything else in his life—in stride. He is ready to deal with what comes next.

"I'm not worried about it. It's just one of those things," he said two days after the end of the 2010 regular season, which also happened to be two days into his run as the manager.

But it had to be strange for a guy who's been so beloved for so long, right? Is it the equivalent of Donnie Baseball getting booed in New York—which, by the way, never happened?

"I had my share of negative press in New York," he said. "There were times when the fans were on me, and the FAN [sports radio station WFAN] was on me. I wasn't doing the job and they wanted see somebody else, whatever. There's no real way to defend that. The only thing you can do is go out and go to work.

"[I'm] really going to be judged by how this club does. [People will say] 'Oh, we should have had this guy,' or, 'This guy would be better,' but you know what? It's all … speculation for me, and I'm not going to get upset with it. I don't worry about it. I don't really read it.

"I knew there was some [backlash], but I don't ever read that stuff for the most part because I don't want to have an attitude with anybody. If you wrote that and you came in tomorrow, I don't want to be so intent on it that I know, *Hey, he wrote that about me* and then I get an attitude with you. I want to treat you the same way today as I treated you yesterday. If you wrote [positively], if you wrote [negatively], if you wrote indifferently. I really want to treat [the press] the same way. I understand that you have a job to do, you may have an opinion. But I don't want to be mad because you don't think [that I did] the right thing.

"Everybody's entitled to that opinion. To me it's going to get down to the bottom line: do I do a good job or not? Period. The end."

There's another bottom line—you just don't know how well or poorly a manager is going to do before he does it.

"There have been quite a few guys—and guys who are having success," said Mattingly, pointing to Piniella, Torre, and Dusty Baker as examples, and, "Bud Black down in San Diego. There are quite a few guys who didn't have that experience. It doesn't mean it's right or its wrong— [Joe] Girardi didn't have any minor league experience.

"Again, I'm not going to sit here and try to defend [myself against] anybody who doesn't like the decision. I'm not really concerned about it. I'm more concerned with doing my job."

And, in a sense, he's been through all this before. After all, if you look up *overachiever* in the dictionary, you might find Mattingly's picture next to it.

"If I was to worry about everybody who didn't think I could do something—that I couldn't run or I didn't have any power or arm strength, [who thought I was] too small for first base, and didn't have enough power for the outfield…if I'm concerned about what everybody says I can't do, then I'm putting my energy into the wrong area."

He laughed when he heard his friend and former manager Buck Showalter say Mattingly has actually been managing his whole life.

"I think anybody who plays the game and wants to win pays attention to what's going on and wonders why," Mattingly said. "I sat out there at first base and thought, *We have to bring in the righty for the guy coming up.* That's not actually doing it but [it's] thinking it, so I'm not really concerned. I want to do a good job. Obviously, I want people to think I did a good job.

191

But that can't be settled now, so I can't be concerned and let anything get in the way of what I've been hired to do. I'm doing the wrong thing already, if I'm going to be bothered by what somebody has to say at this point."

He added that the Dodgers players appear to be ready to play for him.

"It's been fine for me," he said of the reaction. "I think the guys are okay with it. I don't think they're upset with it at all.

"The guys know me. I'm pretty comfortable.... The one thing they can count on that they're going to get from me is that they're going to get the same guy every day. It's not *I come in one day, I've had a good day, and he's good to me*, and then *I've had a bad day and he's treating me like crap*. As a player, it made me sick when a guy treated me differently just because I was hot or cold.

"You learn a lot when you go through tough times as a player. I had some stretches where I didn't swing the bat well, when I hurt my back and I wasn't really putting up any numbers. I could feel the difference when a guy treated me differently, and I never wanted to [be] that guy as a coach. That's been part of what I want to teach and what I bring: they're going to get the same guy every day. They don't get an attitude from me when they're not [playing well] ... I know they're trying. I think it's the one thing that they can count on, and I think they appreciate that."

The day after the season ended, Mattingly, facing the media with general manager Ned Colletti, was asked what he would do if he could do something to change the team's dismal 2010 finish.

"I want this team to have mental toughness," he said.

When asked what went wrong, he said, "It was a lot of areas, really. It takes toughness to play this game. It's not football toughness, where you're banging heads, but you have to get ready to play 162 times, and that is a battle. It is a mental battle to try to get yourself ready every day.

"This year has been an interesting year. It seems like when everything goes bad—and it's nothing I haven't seen before—I felt like we had some guys who are better than the way they played. It's a little different with young guys who have a couple of good years and then a flat year. Sometimes they kind of lose sight of where they're going."

* * *

ESPN contacted former Dodgers manager Tommy Lasorda after the hiring, and even Lasorda said he was a bit surprised at the quickness of the move.

"Yeah, I'm surprised about that," he said. "I've never witnessed that before within the Dodgers organization, but evidently they feel that they know what they're doing and they felt that this guy would be a great manager [for] the Dodgers. So I have to go with that, and I hope that he does well because he's a tremendous guy. He's experienced, he's played. He knows what it's like to play under managers, he's learned a lot from Joe, being his coach. I think it's going to work out well."

However, Lasorda noted that inexperience is something Mattingly has to overcome.

"Don, after all, [has] not had any experience as a manager, so he's going to have to get as much knowledge in as he can before the season starts next year," he said. "That's the thing that he has to do. He's a tremendous guy. I'm wishing him nothing but the best. I'm sorry to see Joe leave— Joe was a tremendous manager. He'll be in the Hall of Fame in five years, and he's done a tremendous job with the Dodgers. So let's hope that Don can continue as the manager of the Dodgers and try to capture that world championship."

Lasorda chuckled when reminded that the Dodgers have had seven managers in 15 years since he left. "When you don't win you have to go, like the rest of us," he said. "In the 20 years that I managed the Dodgers, there were almost 200 managers fired in [Major League Baseball during] that time. If you don't win, it's tough—and today more than ever, you have to win. If you don't win, you fall by the wayside.

"It's very unique for the Dodgers organization, hiring a manager as quickly as they did. They have to give him all the support that he needs, try to get some good ballplayers to help along, and that's what it's going to be. Mattingly is an outstanding gentleman, knowledgeable about the game, and I think he'll make a good manager."

* * *

Amid some of the negative backlash that hit the streets after the Dodgers named Don Mattingly manager for 2011, some of his old friends in New York chimed in with words of support.

"I'm happy that [Torre] gets an opportunity to do it when he wants to do it. [Mattingly] worked hard and put in a lot of time and effort being a bench coach and hitting coach for a long time. Now he's got a chance to manage, and I'm happy for him."

—Derek Jeter

"He is a good baseball man, and I think he will do a very good job for them. One of the positives is that he has been with Joe for a while."

—Alex Rodriguez

"He's followed [Torre] around for a little bit now. Donnie's great. As a hitting coach and being so successful, his work ethic showed me a lot about him. I couldn't believe it that Don Mattingly was my hitting coach, to tell you the truth. I was a big fan of Donnie growing up. Him being there at 1:00 in the afternoon and trying to get us better was special for me."

—Jorge Posada

"[Considering] the time he put in as a hitting coach, he deserves it."

—Tino Martinez

"He knows the game, has a great demeanor, and he has to be helped by working under Joe. Joe had to rub off in a lot of ways.

"He's had a great guy to see and work under, that's for sure. I'm sure he'll do a wonderful job for them. I wish him the best."

—Andy Pettitte

His old pals pointed to Mattingly's communication skills with players as a key ingredient for future success.

"I think that's why as a manager he'll be good," Posada said. "Things that made him really, really good as a hitter—he remembered those things and tried to tweak some of my swing a little bit."

Reached by phone just after the season ended, Mike Pagliarulo, one of Mattingly's close friends in the game, said he wasn't shocked that his buddy got the job and offered a major endorsement.

"I guess you could see things coming down in L.A. You knew something was going to happen at the end of the year, and you knew Donnie was the most likely candidate," Pagliarulo said. "Personally, I think the game desperately needs Don Mattingly and more guys like him.

"Some of the things that are out there and could be improved, you need to tap into that knowledge, that passion, instead of numbers [to improve them].... A guy like Don Mattingly should be at the forefront of that. I believe that's what baseball needs.

"I'm very confident that he can do a great job, but no matter what he does it will be good because the game needs [him]—whether he makes a statement one way or the other, it's going to be the right statement because it's going to be about baseball, pure baseball. That's something I think we desperately need."

Pagliarulo, when asked about the growing feeling before the announcement of Mattingly's hiring that Mattingly *wasn't* going to get the job, said, "Well, you know, there's a reason why the writers have to get out there a little bit earlier than everybody else. Inside the clubhouse we know what's going on a little bit more. I never really felt he wouldn't get a shot at it. I just thought it was a matter of time as to when he was going to get it, but I pretty much thought he was going to get that job. I'm not surprised at all. I don't know where the information [some writers] got [came from], but he followed the right manager, Joe Torre. He's been coaching and [has gained] all kinds of experience and respect and knowledge. I mean, who's better than that?

"He will be honest, whether you like it or not. And he will be ready for that game. You can't control everything during the game, the outcomes are going to be what they are. You can plan all you want, but there's nothing like being ready, and that man was always ready to play. So I know he'll be ready to manage because it's the same game."

* * *

Mattingly spent a good amount of his time after his hiring answering the loads of messages he was getting from friends and even people he didn't know—those who were getting word to him through people he knew.

"I spent quite a bit of time texting guys back," he said. "I've heard from a lot of people. It's been really touching, honestly.

"[Some of the outpouring has come] from different areas than you would think. Not old teammates, just people at home [in Evansville] who say, 'Hey, we were Yankees fans because you were with the Yankees, and now we're Dodgers fans.' People from church, people I don't even know really. They're older, and they were fans of mine when I was playing. They're following me [now], and I didn't realize how closely.

"I've gotten word from some other people saying, 'I've seen a guy at the grocery store. He knows I knew you, and he says he's going to be a Dodgers fan now. He's going to be watching.' It's been really nice, it's been pretty cool.

"You don't realize how many people you know. You stay on your track. I'm here in L.A. now so I don't get to see as many people, so it's really touching [to hear from them]. You forget how many people you have in your life that you don't really realize are part of it."

* * *

Don Mattingly spent the first two days of the 2010 postseason as the first two days of his career as a manager.

"[It feels] good—really good, actually," he said, describing the new experience. "It's exciting—meetings, going over the club, going over our 40-man roster, starting to look at next year."

His staff wasn't complete at the time. According to Mattingly, that was all being discussed. He hadn't moved into the manager's office yet, either—the same one in which Tommy Lasorda used to entertain all his Hollywood pals.

"There's a lot to do, and moving into an office isn't something I'm worried about doing [at the moment]" he said.

He was off to Arizona the following day for his first stint as a manager, running the Phoenix Desert Dogs of the Arizona Fall League. Workouts were due to start and the first game was scheduled for October 12.

He had to know that the Fall League managerial job would come complete with people asking him about the Dodgers. He had been hired less than a month earlier and was off to Arizona as anything but just another veteran baseball guy who was managing a bunch of kids through a 32-game schedule.

After that, Mattingly planned to go home to Indiana. He married Lori Manion in December.

"I'll be back in L.A. a few times, but with our spring training complex there [in Glendale, Arizona, near Phoenix], we're going to have some meetings [during] the Fall League."

He will turn 50 just after the start of the 2011 season, creating a kind of symmetry that goes along with the new job—the job so many said he wouldn't be able to do.

As he said, he's been proving people wrong for a long, long time. Why not one more time?

As the 2010 season ended, along with Torre's stay with the Dodgers, Mattingly and general manager Ned Colletti were already looking ahead.

Mattingly knew there were going to be guys coming back into that Dodgers clubhouse who he was going to have to rely on as he eased into the role of being a rookie manager.

"You like guys that you can count on," Mattingly said. "There are good players and great players, but there are those guys [about whom] you just feel like, *I can count on this guy. He's going to be here ready to play. He'll be on time. He's not going not be a problem. You don't have to worry about him.* It's guys who are tough so that when things are going bad, guys who have that ability to say, 'It's all right. We're going to be okay. It's just something we're going through.' Those guys have that inner confidence and that toughness. They have belief in themselves."

* * *

It took almost two months, but Mattingly's 2011 Dodgers coaching staff was completed in mid-November 2010 with the addition of former Dodgers great Davey Lopes as the first base coach. Lopes hadn't appeared in a Dodgers uniform since being traded in 1982.

"It's a process we looked at very seriously—from the people we brought in and getting the best quality people we could possibly get," Mattingly said. "It was important to bring in people who care about the organization from a historical standpoint but who also want to see us get better at it right now."

Mattingly wanted to keep Bowa as his bench coach, but Colletti thought otherwise, and former Royals manager Trey Hillman was named. Mattingly, speaking to the *L.A. Times*, said, "You know what? It's difficult. I'll say that. I don't know if I want to go much further than that. [Bowa's] knowledge, the way he sees the game is as good as I've seen. It's a difficult situation."

Wallach, who had been seen as a prime candidate to replace Torre, was elevated from managing in the minor leagues to third base coach. Some saw that as a sign Wallach was there to be Mattingly's replacement if things didn't work out. Not that such a thing phased Mattingly.

"I went through that with [Joe] Girardi in New York," Mattingly told the newspaper, speaking of Girardi getting the Yankees job over him. "It's one of those things. It's not uncomfortable for me. I don't think it's [uncomfortable] for him either."

Rick Honeycutt stayed on as pitching coach. Jeff Pentland, who worked under Mattingly with the hitters in '08 and '09, was elevated to hitting coach. Former Dodger righty Ken Howell remained as bullpen coach. In addition, ex-Dodger Dave Hansen was named secondary hitting instructor, and longtime Dodgers favorite Manny Mota was also kept around to help out.

* * *

Finally, we give you a closing thought from our subject, actually offered before he was named manager of the Los Angeles Dodgers:

'To come from where I came from to this point is a long road for the guy who couldn't run, who couldn't throw, and who didn't hit for power," Don Mattingly said. "It's [been] a long ride. It's been a great ride."

Index